Julia Clancy-Smith

Tunisian Revolutions
Reflections on Seas, Coasts, and Interiors

Center for
Contemporary
Arab Studies

GEORGETOWN UNIVERSITY PRESS

ON THE COVER: This image shows the looted villa of Mohamed Sakher al-Materi, Ben ᶜAli's son-in-law, in Hammamet during January 2011 soon after the flight of the president and his entourage. © Marco Salustro/Corbis

Join our mailing list and get updates on new releases and special offers from Georgetown University Press.

Contents

Acknowledgments

The author thanks Osama Abi-Mershed, the director of Georgetown University's Center for Contemporary Arab Studies (CCAS), for the invitation to deliver the annual distinguished Kareema Khoury Lecture in 2012, upon which this essay is partially based; Steven Gertz, the CCAS editor, who guided the project from its origins as a somewhat inchoate public talk to print; Richard Brown, the Georgetown University Press director; and colleagues and members of the audience, who asked tough questions. More thanks are due to the American Geographical Society Library at the University of Wisconsin–Milwaukee, whose rich collection and extraordinarily helpful staff provided additional sources for this essay.

A Note on Transliteration

Consistent transliteration for North African history poses a number of problems because there is no single agreed-upon system. Proper names, place names, and terms for institutions come from a range of languages—classical Arabic, dialectal Arabic, Berber, and Ottoman Turkish. To complicate matters, proper names and place names often came into English through French, which frequently deformed the originals. Therefore, transliteration in this paper is the product of compromise. For the most part, a modified version of the transliteration system in the *International Journal of Middle East Studies* for Arabic is employed. However, only the "ayn" [ᶜ] and "hamza" ['] are indicated. Turkish words, such as *bey* or *dey*, which refer to Ottoman political offices or titles, are used instead of the more accurate Arabic transliteration, *bay*. Arabic words have been given in their singular form, with -s added to the end for plurals. In cases where the plural form is in regular use in English, for examples, *ulama* or *ashraf*, the plural is employed.

Tunisian Revolutions
Reflections on Seas, Coasts, and Interiors

Julia Clancy-Smith

> There has been no "Arab" Spring:
> The perfume of its revolutions
> Burns the eye like tear gas.
> —*Tariq Ramadan, "Egypt: Coup d'État, Act II," 2013*

Introduction

The *port de plaisance* (yacht basin) in the city of Munastir abuts a promontory that still bears the skeletal outlines of a nineteenth-century Italian *fabricca* (fish-rendering factory); not far away are the remains of Punic, Roman, and Byzantine—as well as medieval Islamic, Spanish, and Ottoman—fortresses, businesses, and residences.[1] Clearly, places such as this in the heartland of Africa Proconsularis, as the Roman Empire called its first African colony, have attracted other empires as well as commercial and pleasure interests for millennia. Looming over the promontory today is a five-star tourist complex. When I visited the port of Munastir, now a seaside resort, with a colleague from the University of Tunis in 2009, I noted with satisfaction that the customers for the well-appointed hotels, cafés, and bars were Tunisians as well as "internationals." But it had not always been this way. Four decades ago (when I resided in Tunisia as a Peace Corps teacher), the country's hotel clientele had been almost exclusively French; the "locals" labored as waiters, cooks, maids, and other staff members. Nevertheless, from the late 1970s on, the tourist industry offered women some of the country's first professional management positions; and today, this sector is one of the University of Tunis's most popular majors for both women and men.

The extraordinary expansion of Tunisia's middle class—among the largest in the Arab world—starting in the late 1980s has put family meals and vacations in the country's countless shoreline resorts within reach of many, but not all, of its citizens. Indeed, the emergence of this middle class was intimately tied to international tourism as well as to worker remittances, the country's phosphate industry, and the relocation of light manufacturing from Europe to Tunisia. Needless to say, Tunisia's tourist industry has deeply distinguished it from its Maghribi neighbors to the east and west. One can hardly imagine a vacation advertisement like the following one for Libya even before the 2011 war: "Visitez Tarablis, pays de mer et de lumière" (Visit Tripoli, country of sea and light).

However, Munastir's yacht basin also yielded other data. Most of the luxury vessels in port for winter appeared to be owned by transnationals, judging by their flags and names. Moreover, if one goes slightly inland, the olive groves (whose origins in the distant past can only be imagined) suggested another, quite sinister view of global investment capitalism cum travel industry. Grids of productive trees had been auctioned to the highest bidder and slated for destruction to make way for new villas built for the high-end transnational yachting class. But the 2008–9 global financial and economic crisis and subsequent political unrest severely depressed the tourist industry, which suffered a calamitous drop after the uprisings early in 2011.[2]

As was also true for Carthage and Sidi Bou Saʿid, Munastir had become a potent symbol of the Ben ʿAli regime's excesses even before the country's Jasmine Revolution of 2010–11 because of the palatial compound there occupied by Mohamed Sakher al-Materi, the president's son-in-law. Indeed, luxurious seaside palaces and real estate claimed by the extended Ben ʿAli–Trabelsi clans were among the first political targets after Ben ʿAli's hasty departure in January 2011. Soon thereafter, the National Commission of Investigation into Corruption and Malfeasance (Commission nationale d'investigation sur les affaires de corruption et de malversation) began its work, opening an initial five thousand dossiers into widespread, systemic graft centered upon Mediterranean real estate and the business of tourism.

This essay argues for a *longue durée* approach to Tunisia's unfinished revolutions. As a small excerpt from a larger project in progress, it raises five seemingly disparate questions in search of a coherent framing narrative:

1. When and why did Tunisia become a Mediterranean playground for transnational elites, while its "interior" (the south, border, and central regions) suffered increasing neglect and marginalization?
2. Where and what is the "interior," and how can environmental history deepen understandings of social movements, power, and divergent regionalizations?

3. How did women and gender configure two fundamental identities promoted by the newly independent Tunisian state—secular modernity, and a unique Mediterranean personality?
4. Why was Tunisia, whose prospects for democratic pluralism had seemed the brightest among postcolonial Maghribi states, governed by a populist, single-party regime from 1956 until 1987, and subsequently by a brutal kleptocracy that plundered national resources and further gutted civil society?
5. Finally, if the demands, symbols, targets, and practices of today's mass civic actions draw deeply upon the past, what historical torque do the precolonial and colonial eras exert?

The intent here is less to propose definitive answers to these five questions than to imagine alternatives to the linear nationalist narratives that for the most part continue to serve as the default "container" for North African histories in the contemporary period.[3] Of late, historians and social scientists have come to problematize many conventional (and comfortable) analytical units used in their professions, notably the ideas of the nation-state and of empire. Related concepts—such as distance, scale, and region—have also come under intense scrutiny, generating new thinking on transnationalism and territorialization.[4] Following that lead, this essay explores the historical implications of "coastalization," the progressive (and ultimately unsustainable) concentration of anthropogenic pressures and activities on increasingly vulnerable seas, oceans, and coastal environments worldwide.[5] Some of the greatest threats to the Mediterranean—fossil fuels, pollution, and tourism—have converged upon Tunisia with exceptional force. The ecological crisis in the Gulf of Gabes has earned it the sobriquet "the shore of death" because of its unprecedented outbreaks of environmentally induced illnesses, disappearance of species, and habitat destruction.[6] And the Tunisia–Lampedusa crossing for refugees and/or workers seeking a haven in Europe has become not only a major global human trafficking highway but also a passageway to a watery grave.[7]

For the most part, research on coastalization is mainly driven by the "hard" and interdisciplinary sciences, notably ecology studies, which focus upon urgent contemporary problems, such as hyperurbanization and/or transglobal migrations, and their diverse, often unanticipated, environmental consequences.[8] However, the prehistories of coastalization and its imbrication with states, dominant cultures, and social processes remain largely of secondary interest. For the Maghrib, the shifts of political and economic clout to the Mediterranean or Atlantic coasts have eclipsed ancient inland cities, such as

Constantine, or royal centers of Moroccan legitimacy, like Fez and Meknes, to the benefit of Rabat, Casablanca, Tangier, and Algiers. For Tunisia, the notion of coastalization might appear the least useful, historically speaking. The core of Ifriqiyah (and before that Carthage), which often encompassed eastern Algeria and the maritime zones of western Libya, has for the better part of two millennia remained on the littoral, principally in the Tunis–Carthage–Cap Bon triangle, adjacent to the Sicilian Channel and the central Mediterranean. Nevertheless, the "interiors" also mattered to the state and ruling elites, to the wealth and health of cities, to religious authorities and dissidents, and to trans-sea trade and commerce.[9]

In this essay coastalization represents both an analytical perspective and a heuristic principle that beckon scholars of Mediterranean histories to paradoxically travel far from the alluring, relatively well-documented littoral and into the social worlds of the agriculturalist, farmer, and pastoralist of the semiarid zones before, during, and after colonialism. This perspective/principle reveals how projects, both state-driven and otherwise—such as congresses, transnational education, women's rights, tourism, and international games, beginning in the colonial period (1881–1956)—tipped the balance toward the Mediterranean and away from the plains, mountains, and oases. At the same time, analyzing the transformations of the past two centuries within a framework that is both historical and environmental suggests the complex convergences that produced what is now unsatisfactorily labeled "globalization."[10] It should be explicitly stated from the outset that the present essay concentrates on topics and time periods that have attracted less scholarly attention or were eclipsed by the colonial and/or nationalist narratives.

Preludes and Postscripts: Of Baguettes and Social Protest

The masses of protesters "armed" with baguettes in Tunis's streets in January 2011 during the Jasmine Revolution appeared to signal that economic grievances and household security were principally at stake. However, this myth in the making was quickly dispelled for the international media; the brandished bread actually symbolized quite the opposite.[11] Tunisians could no longer be appeased, as the Ben ʿAli regime and its allied international financial interests had hoped, with consumer culture and middle-class comforts, the latter of which had been sorely undermined by the stupendous venality of the president's family members and party cronies, along with their corporate sponsors. Indeed, after 1990 this venality had gone from "artisanal" to industrial as the neoliberalized economy had opened up vast opportunities for methodical fraud that filled the coffers of foreign banks. State repression, combined with widespread social acceptance of more-or-less voluntary political servitude, undergirded this systemic corruption. Nevertheless, the concepts of "repression" and "corruption" represent an unsteady lens for understanding authoritarianism in the absence of adequate historicization or context.[12]

In a sense, the revolution could have broken out anywhere. Years of both organized and spontaneous acts of civil disobedience all over Tunisia preceded the events of December 2010: public hunger protests, self-immolations, syndicalist agitation, and professional strikes in which lawyers increasingly participated.[13] Indeed, by the turn of the millennium, among the most desperate youth a "culture of suicide" had developed that utterly shocked Tunisian society.[14] It was a cruel irony that the United Nations had declared 2010–11 the "Year of Youth." Yet the final combustive gesture—which was made by a street vendor, Mohamed Bouazizi (or Muhammad Bou ᶜAzizi)—erupted in Sidi Bouzid, a place of no great importance to the outside world or even to many Tunisians, whose identities and interests lie mainly on the coast or overseas. Until 2010 Sidi Bouzid, both the town and the governorate of the same name, attracted few tourists and little notice from Tunis, the country's largest city and capital. However, the region's water resources, nourishing a local food export sector for European markets, had suffered privatization by the Ben ᶜAli regime to cash in on escalating industrial and residential demand in Sfax, Tunisia's second-largest city.[15]

Given that water is an increasingly scarce global commodity, privatized water became even more expensive for family farmers in regions such as Sidi Bouzid. Moreover, "the main centers of water consumption are situated within the coastal region, while water resources are mainly located in the North and in the interior of the country."[16] By the turn of the millennium, the widening rifts between the disadvantaged inland regions (which, despite their diversity, risk being reduced to a caricature with the very notion of "interior") and the urban, cosmopolitan Mediterranean rim could no longer be concealed, much less denied. Today, 80 percent of current national production is concentrated in the coastal areas from Bizerte to Djerba. The provinces of the country's southwest and center-west—which are home to 11 million, 40 percent of the population—only claim 20 percent of its gross domestic product. Indeed, some participants in the Constitutional Assembly put forth proposals in 2012 that they viewed as interrelated: The first demanded that the 1956 Code of Personal Status continue to govern women's rights and status; the second sought to address the problems of the interior.[17]

In the young, but already deeply troubled, twenty-first century, geographers are now sounding the alarm about the specter of coastalization: the hyperconcentration of human activities and state resources on, or adjacent to, the world's major waterways. But this phenomenon, which can be readily perceived in North Africa and around the Mediterranean perimeter, has antecedents from long ago. Thus, we might begin our narrative sometime in the late eighteenth or early nineteenth century, when the waning of the so-called Little Ice Age (c. the sixteenth and seventeenth centuries) brought climatic changes. These transformations intersected with new forms of imperialism, the dramatic expansion of Mediterranean ports, profoundly altered relationships between cities and their traditional hinterlands, and the erosion of village economies and cultures.[18]

Coastalization: Agriculture, Colonialism, and the Granary of Rome

The strategic location of the Carthage–Cap Bon area on the Sicilian channel and its rich agrarian resources had made it a key node in trans-sea exchanges for millennia. By the modern era, Tunisia's economy had been integrated into trade routes and markets located well beyond the Maghrib and the Ottoman Empire.[19] Tunis alone maintained direct commercial ties with the entire Mediterranean Basin, in contrast to the other North African ports, which traded in more restricted zones, such as the Tetouan–Tangiers–Gibraltar corridor. By the late eighteenth century, 60 percent of Tunisia's foreign commerce was with Europe; Marseilles, Malta, and Leghorn were the top three partners.[20]

In large measure, this was the consequence of the European revolutions and the Napoleonic Wars, during which Tunisia had provided foodstuffs and livestock to overseas markets. After 1815, and particularly with France's 1830 invasion of Algeria, Tunisia's coastal provinces and their hinterlands became more firmly enmeshed in trans-Mediterranean, transatlantic, and global exchanges. Indeed, France pressed hard on the beys (regional princes or rulers) to export the "surplus" from agriculturalists in order to feed its huge African army during the decades-long pacification of Algeria. But by then the revolutionary boom years were over. In response, the Husaynid Dynasty (1705–1956) imposed state monopolies on olive and cereal production from the 1820s on, and thus sold future harvests to European buyers—with utterly disastrous results. As crops failed due to recurring droughts, and foreign grain traders reaped profits, Tunisia's economy slid into a long recession, which ironically was due to its deep involvement in Mediterranean commerce.[21] However, little-understood climatic changes in the Mediterranean subregions may have triggered drier growing seasons that endangered rain-fed crop cultivation, particularly in agriculturally marginal zones.[22]

At the same time, both the governing classes and commercial interests gradually turned their backs on the peoples inhabiting Tunisia's western frontier regions and plains.[23] One indicator of their shifting priorities was that by the nineteenth century, the princes of the Husaynid Dynasty no longer chose their wives from the big tribal confederations in order to cement political alliances but increasingly preferred Circassian, Georgian, and especially Italian spouses (or concubines).[24] Nevertheless, the annual *mahalla* (a mobile military unit sent from Tunis under the command of the heir apparent to the Husaynid throne) persisted, although one of its principal functions—assuring justice in the countryside and interior—became less important. Because it functioned as a sort of royal progress, the *mahalla* both conferred and confirmed legitimacy. Long before the Ottoman conquest, the Maghribi states had flexed their muscles and collected revenues by conducting this massive tax-collecting expedition, which laboriously made its way around the country in two annual forays timed for the harvests. But the *mahalla*'s extraction of surplus came to outweigh its dispensing of justice and maintenance of order; in fact, by the 1870s Khayr al-Din Pasha, then the prime minister, had disbanded the *mahalla*. Political elites in Tunis barely controlled their pastoral-nomadic subjects in the border zones with Algeria because the French military had destabilized the western frontiers. Moreover, the organization of a modern army during the 1840s further marginalized the interior's tribal confederations, such as the Wislati and Awlad ʿAyyar, which had long served the state as *makhzan* (auxiliary troops).[25]

State-driven modernization also undermined Tunisia's overwhelmingly agrarian-based economy. In the 1840s the government financed reforms (inspired by the Ottoman Tanzimat decree which reorganized the empire along modern lines) by taxing the peasantry in increasingly abusive ways, and this situation coincided with the country's mounting debt owed to European powers and private lenders. The growing divergence between Tunis and the rest of the country became painfully apparent during the 1864 revolt. The causes of this rebellion—one of the largest, most complex movements in modern North African history—cannot be explained as merely the result of fiscal exactions or foreign interference.[26] They must also be connected to trans-Mediterranean politico-military events, such as the 1848 European revolutions, Italian reunification, and the Crimean War. Another trigger was the erosion of the long-standing religio-moral pacts binding subject with ruler through the dispensation of justice, binding notables of the interior with Tunis elites, and binding city with village. The revolt's repression lasted several years, devastating the farmers of the Sahil (the olive-growing coastal regions) and the pastoralists-cultivators of the central plains and border regions.[27] Thus, long before the onset of French rule, agriculture was already in crisis. Under the French Protectorate (1881–1956), the peasantry did not fare better, despite propaganda that portrayed modern North Africa as the granary of France, as it had been for Rome.

European "investment" in the countryside began during the 1850s, when an unnamed English national sought to introduce cotton cultivation, inspired by similar developments in Algeria and Egypt; this project was abandoned in 1860, as were most rural business schemes attempted by Italian, British, and French entrepreneurs.[28] Usurious loans to the Husaynid Dynasty to underwrite military modernization offered the most spectacular financial gains, as a form of investing in indebtedness. The 1878 forced bankruptcy of the Tunisian state, which was followed by the formation of an international debt commission, constituted an early form of "crisis capitalism," which afflicted Cairo and Istanbul at the same time. For nearly two decades after 1881, French investment in the rural economy was hesitant, if not negligible; servicing Tunisia's international debt and trans-Mediterranean commerce represented the preferred ways of making money. Nevertheless, on the eve of the Protectorate, the French Société de Marseilles purchased a vast agrarian estate at Enfidha near Tunis, the capital city, that covered 90,000 hectares (nearly 350 square miles). And in July 1885 a land use law was promulgated that drew inspiration from the Torrens system of land title registration, which had been first deployed in British South Australia and was also subsequently used in North America and French Algeria to "legally" seize and alienate native properties.[29]

Italian nationals had owned and/or operated numerous small farming estates in Tunisia long before the Protectorate. After 1900 the obsession of the French with the increasingly politicized Italian communities induced a dramatic shift in land and forest policies. Collectively owned tribal properties and Muslim charitable endowments (*awqaf* or *ahbas*), which had been more or less untouched after 1881, were registered and sold off.[30] To offset the substantial Italian presence, Paris vigorously promoted settler colonization, although those French landowners who already possessed large estates in Tunisia proved unenthusiastic about schemes to lure fellow citizens to take up family agriculture. One of the anomalies of agro-imperialism in North Africa was the expansion of highly subsidized viticulture (i.e., the cultivation of vineyards for winemaking), which consolidated European-owned estates into large-scale operations. By 1913 vineyards claimed nearly 18,000 hectares of land and produced wine mainly for local European consumption.[31] This shift from mixed-subsistence to market-oriented agriculture devoted to wine grapes, a crop that the Muslim population did not consume, further undermined village society and endangered local food supplies—unleashing cycles of shortages, and even famines.

This influx of French and French Algerian farmers enjoying hefty subsidies put unbearable pressures upon native peasant and tribal producers to sell rights to land, accept low-paid jobs as rural laborers, or abandon their fields altogether, notably in grain-growing regions. In the olive-producing Sahil, indebtedness to absentee urban landholders grew rampant. And the deterioration of traditional agriculture also caused the near demise of artisanal production, which had depended upon the countryside for raw materials and on rural markets for finished goods. These elements coalesced to pauperize both craftsmen and peasants, and to also exacerbate village-to-urban migrations and rural violence directed against European estates.[32]

The social problems rampant in the Maghrib's countryside partly motivated the convocation of the 1908 Congrès de L'Afrique du Nord in Paris. For ten days, congress participants—who included a handful of Algerian and Tunisian representatives—engaged in scientific debate and raised issues of landholding for native farmers. However, the congress's proceedings report recorded, among other things, the claim that the Torrens Act as applied in Tunisia was not as abusive as it had been in Australia. North African Muslim conference delegates made another important demand—that the colonial regime support girls' education in Arabic—but it fell on deaf or even hostile ears.[33] Five years later, in 1913, students from French North Africa and the Ottoman Empire who were enrolled in French institutions participated in a pan-Arab international congress at the headquarters of the Société de Géographie in Paris. The five-day conference, which attracted a large, diverse group of attendees from as far away as North America, demanded an end to both European and Ottoman political repression.[34]

These conferences, which were held in the Metropole (i.e., on the French mainland), signaled a rupture with the past. One of the hallmarks of the nineteenth century had been the emergence of "universal expositions," or world's fairs, in European capitals to display and celebrate imperial triumphs. However, these 1908 and 1913 conferences served to broadcast and internationalize resistance "from below" to the woes, indeed the sorrows, of the colonies of the European empires.

By the eve of World War I, nationalist unrest in the cities and rebellion in the countryside had reached a fever pitch. As France mobilized Maghribi soldiers by force and guile in 1914, officials in Paris and North Africa feared the worst—mutiny among the "native" troops.[35] Yet the native soldiers remained loyal. Moreover, the North African farmers literally fed the war effort in Europe and the Mediterranean during World War I by exporting great quantities of grain—and this provoked food shortfalls across the Maghrib. At the same time, Tunisians' and Algerians' tax burden was double that of European settlers. During the Great War, Mohamed Bash Hamba, an ardent nationalist who found refuge in Geneva after officials expelled him from Tunis, lobbied for the establishment of native agricultural schools; as he bitterly remarked, "Refusing to open schools that instruct the Tunisian people and provide them with a professional and agricultural education, the French regime instead caters to the needs of the colonial settlers."[36]

The war years and their aftermath amplified three interrelated processes that have heretofore been neglected by historians: the transformation of the Tunisian protectorate into a de facto French colony, the intensification of trans-Mediterranean economic and other exchanges, and the coastalization of power over resource accumulation and distribution.[37]

By the interwar period a rural proletariat had emerged; but most officials ignored its existence.[38] Instead, the École coloniale d'agriculture de Tunis (School of Colonial Agriculture), which had been founded in 1896 to emulate the Institut Agricole d'Algérie (at Maison Carrée, outside Algiers), was refurbished, and its curriculum was revamped after 1923. Despite its importance, this school has aroused little, if any, scholarly interest. Its mission was threefold: to teach innovative farming techniques, to undertake research on agronomy, and to promote French involvement in the rural sector. The school also hired scientists to develop industrial agriculture, notably for olive oil and wine production. In part, its objective was to put to rest the old saw in foreign imperial circles that "France has colonies but no colonists" by luring farmer-citizens from either the Metropole or other parts of the Maghrib. By 1922 France had acquired mandates over Syria and Lebanon; thus training agricultural engineers would not only benefit French North Africa but also these new territories in the eastern Mediterranean. In promotional literature, Tunisia was marketed as a nearby version of Mediterranean France whose climate resembled that of the Midi. The school was cast as a *jardin d'acclimation* for expatriate farmers—who, with their newly minted degrees in hand, would modernize agriculture across the French Empire. In the words of one promoter, the Tunis institute would encourage emigration from France and operate as a "genuine school for colonization that prepared young men to settle in our most distant possessions."[39]

Whatever its success in training hearty farmers for the tropical reaches of

La Plus Grande France, l'École coloniale d'agriculture de Tunis did produce the next generation of the country's small agriculturalists, who had recently migrated to Tunisia from France or elsewhere in the Maghrib; by 1926, 108 students were enrolled. The school grounds boasted laboratories, engineering workshops, a meteorological station, irrigation machinery, and a model farm of 250 acres. The *jardins d'essai* (experimental gardens) were international in scope, notably for breeding and crop development. Animals were imported from parts of the French and even the British empires; for example, Indian or South Asian buffalos and new crops (or strains thereof) were introduced. Significantly, "vernacular" Tunisian Arabic was taught to interested students, indicating that the administration sought to anchor them permanently in Tunisia. Most graduates were either given land allotments of hundreds of hectares or remunerative positions in the public or private sector tied to industrial agriculture or resource extraction.[40]

By the eve of the Great Depression, Tunisia was experiencing a "youth bulge." More than 25 percent of the country's population was under the age of twenty-five years, the mixed blessing of modern, if modest, public health measures. In response to the Depression, massive droughts, and crop failures, the colonial regime subsidized wheat production for export. But it did next to nothing for the Sahil's olive growers, whose trees provided sustenance, directly or indirectly, for one-third of the Tunisian population. In part, the play of local politics informed rural policies—by then Habib Bourguiba, himself from the Sahil, had emerged as the paramount nationalist leader with a populist base in the countryside. Other calculations were also at work; colonial seizures of olive groves had proven more difficult because of the complexity of land use and ownership in this zone of dense, extended family exploitation. But the indebtedness of the olive growers operated as a proxy for "extralegal" land alienation. By the eve of World War II, the inequities in access to agrarian resources had become deplorable. On average, Tunisian farms worked plots of 15 acres on average, and Italians about 100 acres, while French holdings amounted to more than 500 acres.[41]

The war years exerted a tremendous impact upon Tunisia in particular, and thus they need to be factored into investigations of the complex transition from colonial to postcolonial agriculture, a topic thus far ignored by most historians. With independence, both Algeria and Tunisia experimented with various forms of collectivized agriculture. Because of the Cold War, this attracted attention from economic development specialists, who carried out numerous studies but often lacked historical knowledge. After 1956 the new president of the Republic of Tunisia, Habib Bourguiba, followed older colonial policies in part, but favored his home province, the Sahil, over other regions. In contrast to post-1962 Algeria, some European farmers continued to exploit their lands until as late as the Bizerte Crisis of 1961 when Bourguiba imposed a blockade on the French naval base at Bizerte to force France to evacuate this strategic Tunisian port; the confrontation culminated in a three-day battle. Through collectivization, some cultivators acquired rights to abandoned colonial farms or Muslim endowment properties, which had been taken over by the state in 1957.[42] Most significantly for the history of agriculture and the countryside, Mounira Charrad argues that the Neo-Dustur Party's seizure of collective properties held by lineages in the interior marked "the final extinction of tribal politics" in Tunisia.[43]

Collectivization, which was in force between 1964 and 1973, engendered fierce peasant resistance, which further undermined rural production, prosperity, and society. By the mid-1970s, farm exports to mainly European markets did not even cover 50 percent of the cost of imported food. After 1974 state planners abandoned "socialized" agriculture for gradual "free market" strategies, which nevertheless further consolidated large landholdings distributed to loyal Neo-Dustur Party technocrats. Only in the mid-1970s did the Bourguiba regime initiate the first concerted efforts to encourage studies and careers in the agricultural sciences.[44]

Coastalization and Globalization: Tourism, Profane and Sacred

Tourism might seem far removed from the village and farmer; but agriculture and the "grand tour" compete for the same resources—water, land, and labor. Yet variant forms of tourism were intimately tied to coastalization and settler migration from Europe within the larger envelope of imperialism, as exemplified by l'École coloniale d'agriculture. Leisure, travel, and health tourism need to be connected to other kinds of population movements, including missions and militant religious journeys to the land of Saint Augustine. A full historical account of tourism in Tunisia does not yet exist; most studies only address the postcolonial period, which effaces significant historical antecedents.

In 1816 Caroline, princess of Gaul and wife of the heir to the British throne, first introduced modern tourism to North Africa with her visit to Carthage and Tunis, as part of her royal tour of classical Mediterranean sites. From the 1850s on, imperialism and rapidly changing transportation technologies put

Dated 1891, this travel poster illustrates promotional campaigns by the Compagnie Chemin de fer PLM (Paris–Lyon–Méditerranée), or the French railroads, to lure tourists across the Mediterranean Sea to Tunisia. The poster claims that the traveler can leave Paris and arrive in Tunis in 55 hours' time on a "circular voyage" at greatly reduced prices. The visual insert in the right-hand corner shows two historically important congregational mosques in Tunis: In the foreground is the octagonal Ottoman Hanafi mosque founded by Hammuda Pasha in 1655; behind it is the ancient square-towered Maliki mosque, known as the Zaytuna, which was first erected in 698 CE. *Courtesy of Wikimedia Commons*

This travel poster from 1900 was created by the same artist, the French painter Frédéric Alexianu (aka F. Hugo d'Alesi,1849–1906). It displays the city of Algiers as background and proclaims that the Compagnie de Navigation Mixte provides direct service between France, Algeria, and Tunisia. This company was owned by the Société Louis Arnaud, Touache Frères & Cie, founded in 1850. Arnaud had been in the river-shipping business linking Lyon with the Mediterranean and was one of the first to realize that the 1830 conquest of Algiers offered immense opportunities for trans-sea communications. This poster is emblematic of mass tourism marketing because it lures the prospective traveler by offering "reduced prices on ticket packages with the French, Algerian, and Tunisian railroads." *Courtesy of Wikimedia Commons*

This photograph was shot on May 8, 1930, in Carthage on the day that the Eucharistic Congress officially opened. It shows a view of the amphitheater near the site of an excavated Byzantine church where outdoor religious ceremonies were staged. Judging from this image, pilgrims from around the globe, Catholic dignitaries, and other attendees, including journalists, were present. © *Bettmann/Corbis*

The Ben ᶜAli and Trabelsi clans possessed through illegal seizures a number of palaces and villas on the Mediterranean coast. Here looters help themselves to the contents of Ben ᶜAli' s villa on January 24, 2011, in the neighborhood of Soukra in the Tunis region. © *Antoine Gyori/AGP/Corbis*

This photograph captures local Tunisian families with their children as they "tour" the abandoned villa formerly belonging to Mohamed Sakher al-Materi in Hammamet after the fall of the dictator in January 2011. © *Marco Salustro/Corbis*

This rare photograph dates from 1928. It shows a Tunis tramway car being conducted by a Tunisian, which is apparent from the conductor's headgear. The tramway was important in the French colonial period for several reasons. It was the first modern form of transit in the capital city. Second, it was one of the few professions that hired Tunisian workers—in addition to Europeans. Third, the tramway conductors and personnel were among the first to be organized into labor unions, which later became critical to the anti-colonial nationalist movement. Trade unions have historically been (and are today) on the forefront of pro-democracy movements in Tunisia. Finally, this image shows a Tunisian woman wearing a traditional face veil and robe while riding at the front of the tram, which reveals how women moved about the European quarters of the city. *University of California, Santa Cruz, Special Collections, Branson DeCou Collection, MS 38, Photographic Album Series*

Tunisia, French Algeria, and Egypt on the trans-sea mass tourist circuits.[45] This resulted in infrastructural development—hotels, inns, restaurants, cafés, theaters, and the like—and local employment, as well as new forms of leisure and behavior. If tourists to Egypt followed the Nile River Valley deep into the south, travelers in North Africa usually ventured no further than the Roman *limes* (frontiers) because touring the Great Sahara only became feasible in the interwar period. With the birth of archaeology, which was intimately linked with colonialism, knowledge about North Africa's past, above all its Roman and Christian past, was commodified and marketed to entice visitors from Europe and North America.[46] As the heart of Africa Proconsularis, Tunisia had attracted special archaeological interest long before 1881, and the international scientific community regarded excavation findings as "abundant, complete, and far-reaching."[47]

As steam travel gained vogue by the 1870s, bourgeois Europeans and Americans combined excursions to Roman ruins with medical tourism—which included extended winter stays in Algiers or Tunis to enable one to recover from tuberculosis and other ailments. French investors promoted North Africa's ancient hydrotherapy sites as curative way stations for reacclimatizing colonials leaving the French-ruled tropics for the Metropole. In similar fashion, the cities of Egypt, particularly Alexandria, served as decompression chambers for British officials returning from India to the heart of the empire, particularly after the Suez Canal's opening in 1869.[48] By the fin de siècle, wealthy travelers were purchasing first-class tickets from the Parisian Pacquebots Tonache, boarding the rapid night train from the Gare de Lyon to Marseille, and sailing to North Africa in forty hours or so.

However, the belle époque for tourism began when the Tunisia Palace Hotel opened its doors in 1902, claiming the rank of the "most beautiful resort on the African coastline." Boasting more than one hundred rooms and furnished apartments, the Palace offered French cuisine, fine wine cellars, electricity, gardens, telephones, and hydrotherapy; "all of its rooms were exposed to sunlight."[49] Franco-British international touring rivalry explains the organization of the French Tourism Committee in 1903. Advertisements in the 1908 edition of Thomas Cook's *Tourist Handbook for Switzerland* touted another establishment in Tunis, the Grand Hotel, which had a specific clientele in mind. *Handbook* readers were assured that it boasted electric lights, a lift, and was situated in "the healthiest and most central position of Tunis. With 150 rooms, full south, hall, smoking, writing, music, and reading room with English and foreign papers," the establishment guaranteed "perfect sanitary arrangements."[50] Whether arriving by steamer from Malta or via the train from

Algeria, travelers were met by the hotel's omnibus and staff. Most crucially for mass tourism, this hotel accepted Cook's coupons. Mediterranean Africa represented the perfect spot for regaining one's health, thanks to the science of medical climatology, packaged tours, and the revolution in communications epitomized by the telegraph. Colonial officials, investors, archeologists, and physicians assumed leading roles in promoting the transnational movement of people from north to south.

Hotel clients reflected the capital city's growing cosmopolitanism, as well-heeled tourists, bankers and pashas of international finance, and shrewd entrepreneurs poured in. However, not all newcomers were wealthy; impoverished subsistence migrants from the islands had relocated to Tunisia as early as the 1820s. By 1900 the large volume of ship passengers debarking in La Goulette—due to predictable, fairly cheap transportation—created job opportunities. The multilingual Maltese residents of Tunisia filled the growing demand for translators and guides. Thus, intersecting pull and push factors combined to convince many Europeans to leave home for North Africa—the lure of the exotic, the desire to flee personal or political difficulties, dreams of striking it rich, and, for Christian missionaries, the desire to proselytize the "heathens."[51] The most dramatic instance of missionary tourism arose during the interwar period, and it reveals the close meshing between internationalized touring, on one hand, and religion and politics, on the other.

In 1930, as part of the Centenary of French Algeria, the International Eucharistic Congress was convened in Carthage. However, these paired displays of France's glory differed substantially. Algeria indulged in noisy celebrations of empire, the army, and colonial science; and, though tourist promotion was ramped up, it tended toward the profane. Tunisia, in contrast, hosted a militant reaffirmation of Christianity's long historical roots in North Africa. The first Eucharistic Congress had taken place in Lille in 1881 to defend the Church against the Third Republic's anticlericalism; subsequent congresses were convened in France or the Catholic regions of Europe. The Carthage affair was the first and only time that a colonial state with a large Muslim population hosted this international gathering.[52] The timing could not have been less fortuitous—during the onset of failed harvests and global economic crises.

The Protectorate's authorities approved the Church's requests for the Eucharistic Congress's venue after intense negotiations with the Quai d'Orsay (as the Foreign Ministry is known) in Paris. Ahmad Bey II (who reigned 1929–42) agreed, albeit halfheartedly, to serve as honorary president; taxes imposed upon Tunisians partially bankrolled the festivities. It is unlikely that Muslim officials serving the Protectorate had any inkling of how this commemoration—overseen by Alexis Henri Cardinal Lépicier, and dedicated to "the Eucharist in Africa's Testimony"—would be staged.[53] Paradoxically, the Carthage pilgrimage enjoyed the full support of President Gaston Doumergue (1924–31), the only Protestant to hold that office, and of the resident-general, François Manceron (1929–33), who had previously served as a high-ranking official in the region. Neither Paris nor Tunis appeared uncomfortable with patronizing an event that violated France's 1905 laws of church/state separation, although Pope Pius XI had designated Carthage as the chosen site three years earlier.[54] Significantly, Louis Bertrand, the Algerian writer and anti-Islamic polemicist, had proposed Carthage for a future Eucharistic Congress as early as 1914 in his tract *Le sens de l'ennemi* (*The Sense of the Enemy*), when he asserted: "We are at home in Carthage, where we have nothing to fear from Islamic susceptibilities."[55]

In addition to muscular faith, material considerations were at work; entrepreneurs anticipated financial windfalls for transporting, housing, and feeding 25,000 pilgrims from around the world.[56] Delegations hailed from Europe and the Americas; and Armenian, Syriac, and Melkite Catholics, then under French rule in the mandates, formed an "Oriental Section." A US delegation of one thousand participated; but the "polyglot nature of the Congress seemed to annoy" many of them, so they went sightseeing instead for Roman or "oriental" souvenirs. In response to the massive influx, the locals set up food and drink stands and peddled "knicknacks" and "gewgaws"; "Tunisian wine merchants, beer dispensers, restaurateurs, and shopkeepers stayed open for 24 hours per day."[57] To assure social order, Senegalese troops were imported from Dakar to act as colonial police units and traffic cops to deal with the frightful congestion on the road between Tunis and Carthage.

A major challenge for the organizers of the Eucharistic Congress was room and board. The vast majority of participants resided on board ships in the harbor (in a manner reminiscent of today's cruise lines), but several thousand pitched tents on private land that had been provided without charge by a Tunisian Jew. Calls went out to respected Tunis families to welcome elite pilgrims into their homes. The *shaykh* of the municipality and other urban officials inventoried Muslim households willing to accommodate foreign notables. The princesses of the Husaynid family opened their seaside palaces to Catholic prelates and pilgrims. One of the princes made room at private family residences for members of the congress's organizing committee; Tunisian Jews of means offered the same kind of hospitality. Several princesses who were enrolled at the Catholic White Sisters' school requested permission to attend the festivities. The roll call of Tunis dignitaries on congress committees—for example, Sidi Ahmad Bayram, *shaykh al-Islam*; and Sidi Tahar ibn al-ʿAshur, *bash mufti*—hints that Protectorate officials engaged in feverish behind-the-scenes arm-twisting to legitimate the congress.[58]

Political calculations undergirded the ecumenical gestures that were made to include Italians and Maltese Catholics in the festivities; the former were permitted to form their own "national section." This may have represented an attempt by secular colonial officials to politically neutralize the Italians of Tunisia and to offset the growing appeal of hypernationalist, trans-Mediterranean fascism, which had become increasingly allied with the conservative, internationalist branch of Catholicism. Clerical organizers in Tunis relied, however reluctantly, upon modern means of communication—radio microphones—and even consented, after tense negotiations, to allow US newsreel operators to film on the altar, where the red-clad papal legate conducted the Solemn Mass.[59] *Time* magazine reported that "the pageantry was as magnificent as only Eucharistic Congresses can be—French soldiers, Zouave bands shrilling and drumming native marches, cardinals, archbishops, bishops (100), priests (4,000). . . . Orientals, Europeans, 400 altars, 200 tons of wax candles, the Papal colors white and yellow everywhere."[60] Staged to overawe even the most indifferent believer, the congress targeted Catholic audiences around the globe. However, a second audience may have been anticlerical politicians in France, who could hardly fail to appreciate the Church's international mobilizing power—in a Mediterranean imperial possession, no less.

The Eucharistic Congress's organizers drew upon archaeological excavations in Carthage that first the French missionary society the Missionaries of Our Lady of Africa, known as the White Fathers, and then the Protectorate's Antiquities Office had been working on for decades. These had brought to light stunning Christian Roman and Byzantine basilicas as well as the shrines of African martyrs. Indeed, martyrdom and the demonization of Islam went hand in hand. As Solemn Masses, processions, and liturgical musical events took place across the capital city, posters in several languages announced that the Crusades had recommenced. Thousands of European children, both resident and foreign, carried palm fronds through the streets, their crusaders' robes emblazoned with large crosses; one source claimed that many of these "little singing children in white" were recent converts from Islam (perhaps orphans). During his official sermon, the papal legate, Cardinal Lépicier, characterized Islam's historical impact upon the Maghrib as nothing but "fourteen centuries of ruin and death."[61] This he did with the Husaynid family, ulama dignitaries, and Tunisians, many of whom served the Protectorate, in attendance.

The response was swift and unequivocal. Students at Zaytuna University and Sadiqi College boycotted classes and clashed in the streets with the police, who then dragged them before French magistrates. National outrage dramatically reshaped older political alliances and compromises; for instance, one wing of the Tunisian ulama that had remained "neutral" or accommodating to the Protectorate now openly joined the nationalist movement. The old notables of Tunis, whose reputations had been irrevocably tied to the Eucharistic Congress when their names appeared in the French and Arabic newspapers, were now discredited. Soon a new generation of men from the Sahil, many educated in Franco-Arab schools in Tunisia or in the Metropole, came to the political foreground.[62] Indeed, Habib Bourguiba, leader of the Neo-Dustur Party and the first president of Tunisia (1956–87), claimed to have experienced a political epiphany during the furor generated in 1930. Though he was not present at the congress, Bourguiba returned to Tunis from Paris (where he had earned a French law degree) soon thereafter to discover that employment was difficult to secure for a Muslim subject.[63]

However, anticolonial activism did not originate with Bourguiba, despite the later myth of the nation's "great founding father." Organized urban workers had struck against unpopular Protectorate policies even before World War I, notably on the Tunis tramways, which employed both Italian and Tunisian workers.[64] In 1919 a section of the main French labor union admitted "natives" but only at an inferior rank. The Confédération Générale des Travailleurs Tunisiens, which was formed in 1924, represented the second-oldest "native" labor union in all of Africa. The Confédération Générale was replaced in 1945 by the Union Générale Tunisienne du Travail, which has continued to play a critical role in organized political action. Mining was one of the first sectors of the economy to be developed. In 1885 French geologists discovered vast phosphate and lead ore deposits in the interior; four years later, the Compagnie de Phosphate et de Chemin de Fer de Gafsa began exporting commercial quantities of the mineral so valuable for agricultural fertilizer, and this activity drove railroad construction linking the interior to Mediterranean ports. By the 1930s an industrial labor force (which also included Italian workers) had matured in the interior's mining zones, notably in the phosphate-rich city of Gafsa, where a local theater of protest crystallized; militants from the Neo-Dustur movement communicated anti-French grievances to the populace through plays and satirical productions.[65]

The spatial coordinates of the protests triggered by the Eucharistic Congress demonstrate the maturation of trans-Mediterranean political agitation and the existence of critical migration corridors. North African diasporic communities in Europe long predate independence. Labor shortages during World

War I drew (or forced) thousands of North African men to migrate to France in order to toil in factories or serve the colonial army. Though most returned home, some stayed as industrial workers in the Metropole. Just as significantly, educational institutions in Paris and other French cities attracted increasing numbers of North African students, including members of Jewish minorities and some women. As Bourguiba's educational trajectory illustrates, globalization and coastalization were mutually reinforcing because families from the provinces relocated to Tunis to place their children in school there, from whence some went off to the Metropole for advanced studies.[66] Another case in point is Elie Fitoussi, a member of the Young Tunisians and leader of the local Jewish community. In 1898 Fitoussi left to study law in Paris, where he received his degree in 1901. He subsequently pursued a highly successful legal career representing transnational business interests and traveled for decades between Aix-en-Provence and Tunis. In 1930, as the backlash to the Eucharistic Congress unfolded, he published an important work on the Tunisian state.[67]

Via the international press, word of the Eucharistic Congress crossed the Mediterranean to Maghribi workers and students' associations in France; they dispatched outraged telegrams to Tunis decrying the Crusade against Islam (and also Judaism). Telegrams, petitions, and signed letters of approbation appeared in the French and Arabic newspapers around Tunisia. (One might argue that they represented the new social media of the day.)[68] Catholic enthusiasts had calculated that the Eucharistic Congress would unify the Church; but the opposite occurred. Some members of the White Fathers openly sided with Tunisian nationalists in denouncing the congress as an imperial pilgrimage cum tourism "crusade."[69]

If the Carthage event proved a boon to nationalists across North Africa and in France, another stupendous colonial misstep five days after the Eucharistic Congress ended further internationalized anticolonial sentiment. In Morocco the Berber Zahir (Decree) of May 1930, promulgated to divide the Berbers from the Arabs through legal manipulations, confirmed suspicions that Islam was under siege. Indeed, the Zahir elicited protests from both Egypt and Syria, where nationalist leaders condemned the Protectorate's policies.[70] Under Bourguiba's leadership the New Dustur Party, which commanded immense popular support in the countryside, in 1933 for the first time demanded total independence from France.[71] If l'École coloniale d'agriculture had accentuated Tunisia's Mediterranean nature to attract potential student-farmers and settlers from the Metropole, the 1930 Eucharistic Congress had demonstrated that globalization, colonialism, and coastalization intersected on multiple levels but in unanticipated ways. Finally, the redeployment of troops from West

Africa to Tunisia demonstrates the growing mobility of imperial policing and colonial violence.[72]

As the Great Depression, agrarian disasters, and famines ravaged the Maghrib, unprecedented 1931 floods in eastern Algeria and Tunisia's Majarda River Valley brought more misery but also fed nationalist fervor. In addition, the social response to these inundations hastened the crystallization of Muslim women's organizations in Tunis. Another international assembly two years after the Eucharistic Congress championed a transnational feminine identity— one ostensibly unsullied by the divisions of politics, state, and religion.

Mediterranean Women, Politics, and Islam

From a comparative perspective, the legal, social, and political condition of women fundamentally distinguishes postcolonial Tunisia from Algeria and Morocco. One of Bourguiba's major boasts was that in 1956 he had liberated Tunisian women, principally through education and legal reforms, from colonial and religious oppression. As current research on gender and empire has abundantly demonstrated, women were central to modern imperial projects worldwide; together, colonial and gender studies have transformed the historiographies of the Middle East and North Africa.[73] Not surprisingly, the French regimes in Algeria and Tunisia manipulated Muslim women's status, either to deny political representation to native men and/or to promote a positive image of colonialism. Earlier research on Algerian Muslim and Jewish women, or European "settler" women, tended to analyze gender relations, hierarchies, and policies within the frame of the colonial state, which severs French Algeria from transnational processes in the Maghrib, the Middle East and North Africa, and the Mediterranean.[74]

A new forum on "the woman question" from the interwar period illustrates one of this essay's major arguments about the growing torque of coastalization. In March 1932 the first Congrès des Femmes Méditerranéennes was convened, somewhat counterintuitively, in the interior city of Constantine.[75] Its mandate was to bring together in harmony representatives from the countries rimming "La Grande Bleue" (the Mediterranean).[76] This particular meeting may have emulated the May 1923 International Women's Suffrage Alliance, held in Rome, in which the Egyptian feminist Huda Sha'rawi (1879–1947) not only participated but also gave a speech on rights in Egypt.[77]

Curiously, Switzerland sent one of the largest delegations because it argued that the Rhône River's headwaters originated in the Swiss mountains, thus making their nation part of the Mediterranean region. However, the Geneva-based League of Nations' keen interest in female rights probably explains the participation of thirty-one Swiss women led by a Madame Debret-Vogel. Another organization with ties to Geneva, the International Alliance of Women for Suffrage and Equal Citizenship, commissioned one of its members, Massara Kélani of Syria, to report on "native" women under the French Mandate.[78] Attendees hailed from Spain and Italy, as well as nations far removed from the Mediterranean, such as Romania. The press took special note of the participation of Adji Pasha, an elected member of the Turkish Assembly, because at that time some European nations, particularly France, had not yet granted women the vote.[79]

At the congress, the participants subjected to intense scrutiny various national and transnational issues that feminists and their organizations had long publicized—the nationality of women married to foreigners in their respective nations of origin, maternal and child protection, prostitution, girls' education, female suffrage, and the right to work. According to the Algerian writer and activist Marie Bugéja, the meeting's goal was to achieve "*une action humanitaire féconde*."[80] Her résumé of the proceedings drew upon the language and ideology of human rights, which characterized the League of Nations' positions on a range of social problems worldwide. An array of projects and agendas swirled around this unusual (for the time) congress, whose female attendees, though principally haute bourgeoisie, did not necessarily agree on objectives or strategies. The aims of the colonial bureaucracy remain opaque, although high rollers were in attendance—including the governor-general, who officially opened the congress; the prefect and mayor of Constantine; municipal councilors; and a host of other officeholders.

Participants, journalists, and onlookers, among them some Muslim North African men, took part in heated discussions, although no Algerian Muslim women assisted at the sessions (as far as we know). Nevertheless, these women were constantly evoked during the conference. Officials in Algiers and Paris must surely have been dismayed by the series of resolutions passed to "uplift" the Algerian woman through changes to Islamic *and* colonial laws, policies, and practices governing marriage, divorce, and education. Delegation members lauded Tunisian efforts to improve women's condition through their own (i.e., outside colonial control) initiatives in order to shame reluctant French officialdom and "conservative Muslims" in Algeria into action.[81]

For our purposes, the Congrès des Femmes Méditerranéennes was momentous because of its framing within a supranational geocultural imaginary, the Mediterranean, which was employed in order to debate women's rights in the emergent language of human rights. Indeed, one detects the outlines of a nascent "Mediterranean universalism," which offered a subterfuge for *not* talking about Muslims on the sea's southern and eastern shores. Nonetheless, claims about a "Mediterranean personality" had a longer pedigree; it had been first articulated in French Algeria in about 1900 to distinguish European colonials from Algerian Muslims and the "effete" French of the Metropole.[82] In the postcolonial era, the ideology of "Mediterraneanism" was reinvigorated and put to similar as well as other uses by both Bourguiba and Ben ʿAli.

In comparison with Algeria, colonial discourse on, and policies toward, Tunisian women were marked by contrasts and similarities, parallels and intersections. (Needless to say, the notion of "women" represents a huge construct that demands social, religious, and temporal disaggregation.) However, a critical difference was that girls' education and schooling in various forms became increasingly available *before* 1881 in Tunisia, which itself was a product of the country's deeper and wider integration into trans-Mediterranean circuits of exchange. As a result, colonial officials never enjoyed the tight (and harmful) grip upon access to learning that marked education in Algeria. Although the Protectorate attempted to stage-manage education, for example, by publicizing in international arenas the 1900 establishment of the School for Muslim Girls in Tunis (which was financially supported by Muslim reformers and some families as well as the resident-general's office), it could never control social demand and therefore outcomes. Thus, somewhat ironically, this showpiece for girls' schooling in the French Empire educated the wives of many Tunisian nationalists, including Tawhida bin Shaykh (1909–2010), who later graduated with a medical degree from Paris in 1936, the first North African woman to become a physician. As a pioneer for women's health and reproductive rights during the interwar period, bin Shaykh was a nationalist in her own fashion.[83]

During the 1920s a feminist movement coalesced in the capital city. A watershed event came in 1924, when Manubiya Wartani, a young Muslim woman attending a public conference in Tunis on women's rights, removed her veil and addressed the audience in a manner reminiscent of Huda Shaʿrawi's defiant public unveiling in the Cairo train station in 1923. In 1930 the scholar of Islam Tahar Haddad (1899–1933) published his manifesto for women's emancipation, *Imra'tuna fi al-shariʿa wa al-mujtamaʿ* (*Our Women in Islamic Law and Society*), which stirred up acrimonious debates within conservative ulama ranks and cost Haddad his Zaytuna University post.[84] Improvements in female status in Egypt and in Turkey inspired Haddad to demand an end to polygamy, repudiation, and the veil (which he likened to a muzzle) and to advocate girls' education. At the same time, the Husaynid household incubated new forms of female associational life. During the terrible 1931 floods, the princesses and palace women instituted a charitable association to assist desperate families. During these same years, robust labor and nationalist movements appeared in Tunisia, somewhat in contrast to Morocco and Algeria.[85]

By World War II several women's organizations had been established in Tunis. Bachira Ben M 'Rad, whose father was a leading nationalist, founded the Muslim Union of Tunisian Women; and Nabiha ben Milad and Gladys ʿAdda cofounded the Union of Women of Tunisia (UFT), which recruited members from families belonging to the Communist and Socialist parties. Among the Muslim Union's objectives was to provide educated Tunisian women with access to teaching posts and to organize girls clubs, including a girls' section of the Scouts. The UFT, which has received less scholarly attention, sought to ameliorate conditions for North African soldiers fighting in Europe and to address wartime shortages of basic supplies and foodstuffs in parts of Tunisia that were ravaged by Allied-Axis bombardments and military campaigns. With the cessation of hostilities, the UFT pressed for clinics to redress the colonial regime's neglect of women's health and education, because nearly nine-tenths of Tunisian women remained unlettered.[86] Illiteracy impeded not only personal social mobility but also physical mobility; social disapproval of women's displacements, even for educated urban women, was still the norm. These two elements together conspired to concentrate women's rights activism in the capital city and to inhibit the growth of a truly mass movement "from below" elsewhere in the country, in contrast to the male nationalist organization.

After the war the UFT agitated with other groups for Tunisia's independence from France and democracy. It petitioned the Parliament in Paris to demand civil and human rights for Tunisian political prisoners incarcerated in colonial prisons. With the outbreak of the Algerian Revolution in 1954, UFT women supplied medical and financial support to Algerian combatants who traveled clandestinely to Tunisia for assistance—in a period when France's army still occupied Tunisia.[87] No historical study exists of North African women's experiences during and immediately after World War II. However, it can be argued that the disruptions and hardships of the war paradoxically served to legitimate female rights campaigns, a pattern seen in other parts of the globe, although violence and disorder can block or destroy opportunities for women.

With Tunisia's independence came a second watershed—the August 1956 promulgation of the Code of Personal Status (CPS), the most progressive family law code in the Middle East and North Africa (with the exception of Turkey). According to Mounira Charrad, the CPS "placed the country at the forefront of the Arab world in regard to women's rights."[88] It abolished polygamy and repudiation, instituted judicial divorce, and declared legal equality of the sexes; and in the following decades, it was continuously amended. The initial motivations for, and social response to, the CPS were extremely complex. The CPS and women's history in the post-1956 period have benefited from extensive research and analysis; thus, it is unnecessary to narrate that story here. Of significance, however, is the fact that as soon as the CPS was legislated, Bourguiba formed the National Union of Tunisian Women (l'Union Nationale de la Femme Tunisienne), "merging" the other women's associations into this union, which was paired with the single party, the Neo-Dustur. Thus, state feminism was launched, and it endured for much of Bourguiba's presidency. Only in the 1980s did a new generation of feminists dare critique the interpretation and application of the CPS and seek autonomy from the ruling party. However, a cruel paradox hindered feminist objectives. The colonial "law of associations" from the early 1900s remained in force; thus, organizations not enjoying formal state recognition were forbidden.

Bourguiba, and his successor Ben ʿAli, managed women's rights as a political hedge fund against national and, above all, international accusations of the abuse of human rights. Marzouki coined the ironic and brilliant term "alibi women" to argue that postcolonial regimes across the Maghrib indulged in these maneuvers.[89] As Tunisian feminists have long observed, party elites excelled at disseminating propaganda with soothing messages about modernity for European audiences who touted the relatively (and undeniably) better legal status of women: "Every foreign guest, each diplomatic delegation or international meeting in Tunisia was provided with ample documentation regarding female rights and progress."[90] Though a national holiday (August 13) celebrates the passage of the CPS in 1956, not all members of society regard this revolutionary legislation as a pillar of the "Tunisian personality."[91] In fact, during debates over the new Constitution since 2011, Article 28, governing women's status, has proved the most contentious.

In 1985 the Islamist Movement (Harakat al-Ittijah al-Islami, or Islamic Tendency Movement) demanded a national referendum on the CPS, which it equated with state-enforced secularization. The movement argued that the CPS not only violated the religiously sanctioned existence of gendered complementary spheres for men and women but also deprived men of employment by legislating gender equality in the workforce.[92] Its successor, and the winner of the 2011 Constituent Assembly elections, the Renaissance Party (Al-Nahda, or Ennahda), holds more or less the same view. The debates that raged until 2014 about the place of women's rights and religion in the new Constitution and in public education—especially at the University of Tunis's

Manouba Campus, the largest in the system—bear witness to this.[93] Therefore, it might be argued that the Tunisian feminism—mainly urban, middle-class, and "secular"—that is enshrined in the 1956 CPS was largely a product of historical processes concentrated in the capital city region and on the coasts that converged with globalization.

Mediterranean Games, Politics, and Dissent

The Bourguiba and Ben ʿAli regimes systematically promoted Tunisia's allegedly "unique" Mediterranean identity in a discourse that mimicked the tourist industry's advertisements, but in multiple venues.[94] In addition, both presidents raised the specter of Algerian political Islam in order to justify denying citizens a genuine voice and vote in a truly multiparty system. A Mediterranean national personality, however, served a crucial discursive and political function similar to the 1932 Women's Congress—it occluded Islam and the fact that Muslims now resided in large numbers within Europe itself. However, enthusiastic promotions of a maritime identity made good business sense, particularly given the slick Madison Avenue packaging of the world into a "global beach" by the late twentieth century. In response, the number of international festivals in Tunisia proliferated, by 2008 reaching nearly fifty, the vast majority of which were held in seaside venues. Moreover, the oases, especially Tozeur, hosted numerous Saharan-themed events to coincide with the European winter vacation season.

From the 1950s on, mass tourism to the Mediterranean Sea's southern rim accelerated and introduced new sports to North Africa. It also enlarged the popularity of "traditional" sports—such as wild boar hunting, wrestling, and soccer, the last introduced under the Protectorate—which until very recently were coded as exclusively male. To these were added tennis, volleyball, basketball, and other sports, notably golf, which tends to attract a high-end clientele, both Tunisian and international. To date there has been scant historical literature on the evolution of sports in Tunisia starting in the colonial period. Omar Carlier's research on French Algeria established significant connections between local sports clubs, some of which admitted both European and North African players, the growth of syndicalism, and the emergence of civil society in the early twentieth century.[95] Thus, it is necessary to triangulate between modern sports, nationalism, and internationalism or globalization.

However, the Tunisian trainer, sports teacher, and scholar Borhane Erraïs (1935–2013) submitted a dissertation in 1992 devoted to the history of Tunisian sports largely during Bourguiba's presidency.[96] Though soccer remains the sport par excellence, Erraïs's personal odyssey indicates that basketball had caught on even before independence, in the late 1940s or early 1950s. Erraïs hailed from the Tunis nobility, and his biography indicates that sports associations, such as the Saint-Germain Club, that were in existence under the Protectorate had included players of diverse backgrounds. By 1957 the Étoile Sportive de Radès had become the leading basketball club and was completely Tunisian in composition; thus sports and national unity were mutually reinforcing. Moreover, many clubs formed during the Protectorate were tied to trade unionism, a pattern seen elsewhere. For example, the Tunisian tramway workers (*traminots*) had long organized their own teams and matches. Erraïs went on to become the president of the Tunisian Federation of basketball, and between 1967 and 1970 he served as director of the prestigious Institut National des Sports. Also important is the fact that he advocated women's sports, as indicated by his publications and participation on international committees. He and other physical trainers contended that traditional gender norms across the Mediterranean, less than Islam per se, had impeded social acceptance for female sports.[97] At the same time, he played in the 1957 Pan-Arab Games and in the 1959 Mediterranean Games.

During the Cold War international sporting events outside the Olympics cycle gained importance and drove the tourist industry. The brainchild of the Egyptian Muhammad Tahar Pasha, the first Mediterranean Games were held in Alexandria in 1951 to bring together youth from different continents, religions, and cultures. However, as with the 1932 Women's Congress, politics overrode geography because players from states not adjacent to the sea (e.g., Andorra and Serbia) were allowed to participate, while others were not (Palestine and Israel). Since their inception, only Turkey and Tunisia have twice hosted the Mediterranean Games. These sporting extravaganzas—convened by Bourguiba in 1967, and by Ben ʿAli in 2001—were intended in part to undercut internal dissent and to parade the country's modernity.[98]

In the months preceding the 2001 games, the Tunis region resembled a vast, feverish construction site as the government scrambled to make ready for thousands of teams, athletes, spectators, and journalists. Yet all was not well. One thorny issue was where to locate the foreign press corps' headquarters; predictably, journalists were quarantined away from downtown Tunis in a controlled media center on the Lac de Tunis. In those very same months, human rights activists, who had retreated into fear during the harsh repression of the 1990s, were emboldened by the presence of the international press corps. The Tunisian Human Rights League (Ligue Tunisienne des droits de l'Homme), founded in 1977, which is the oldest branch in the African or Arab worlds and has many women members, again dared to hold meetings; in 2001 some league activists even consented to brief foreign reporters on media suppression. And directly connected, the families of political prisoners sought out international journalists and human rights monitors.[99]

Meanwhile, the regime's seizures of prime Mediterranean real estate became more brazen. In 2001 the old colonial hotel in La Marsa, the Zephyr, which had been abandoned for years, was expropriated from its rightful owners under shady circumstances and leveled to the ground; an American-style shopping mall rose in its place. Ben ʿAli's extralegal property foreclosures became the focus of intense, if discreet, conversations and whispers among denizens of seaside suburbs while socializing at home or on the beach. In retrospect the turn of the millennium appears to have constituted another memorable year like 1930, as democratic mobilization outside governing structures converged with Mediterranean universalism and transnational forces—or coastalization—through complex circuits, and with unintended results.

From Sidi Bou Saʿid to Sidi Bouzid: Targets and Symbols

The historical weight of the Mediterranean villa in the collective Tunisian consciousness is undeniable; its origins date to the medieval Hafsid period, if not to Carthage. After the forced departure of BouʿAzizi's family members from their town in 2011, street rumors in Sidi Bouzid claimed that they were being housed in a Tunis villa, which further enraged the townspeople. This might appear immaterial, but it is not, when interpreted through a long-term historical lens. We need only recall the 1930 Eucharistic Congress, when the Husaynid princes and princesses opened their palaces to visiting dignitaries. Further back in time, the beys had consciously pursued "villa diplomacy" during the nineteenth century by loaning their beautiful residences to the representatives of bigger, meaner states. Yet these splendid structures, once architectural expressions of privilege and notability, were now associated with subservience to outside rule. The La Marsa Convention, imposed by a French army in 1883, was signed at the bey's palace by the sea, thereby establishing the Protectorate. After deposing the Husaynid Dynasty in 1957, Bourguiba ordered the demolition with dynamite and backhoes of many Husaynid palaces and gardens in La Marsa to erase the landscapes of memory.[100]

The globalized liberal economy of the 1990s generated new social expectations and disparities, epitomized by the lavish houses mushrooming on the shoreline of La Marsa, Carthage, and Sidi Bou Sa‘id, the jewel of the North African coast. Luxury as well as mass international tourism (after 1989, increasingly from Eastern Europe) soared, furnishing hard currency and employment, but also fueling religiocultural discontent. This was true not only in the "interior" but also in the vast *bidonvilles* ringing downtown Tunis—neighborhoods such as Douar Hichar in the Manouba suburb—that had long housed the urban poor as well as recent arrivals from the countryside. Immediately after the "medical coup" of 1987 that installed Ben ‘Ali in power, construction began on a superlarge, Walmart-sized palace in Sidi Dhrif, close to Sidi Bou Sa‘id, where the American ambassador's magnificent residence also stands.

As the new president's quite garish palace went up on land whose legal status remained murky, the security presence in the area reached alarming proportions. The locals, who had long been accustomed to strolling along the gentle hill overlooking the water, now experienced heightened intimidation and even interrogation. Other immense villas housing members of the Trabelsi clan dotted the coast from Tunis to Munastir. In 2007 Leila Trabelsi purchased a palace on the marina in Hammamet measuring more than 3,000 square meters for the absurdly small sum of €50. Much of this real estate had been *mulk al-dawla* (state properties), or privately owned family plots confiscated for their view. In effect these structures represented highly visible, concrete expressions of the simultaneous elaboration of the murderous "secret" police state and its architecture of oppression and expropriation. Just before Bou ‘Azizi set himself ablaze late in 2010, the news spread across Tunis that the Trabelsi clan was poised to privatize the Parc Belvédère, the city's largest and oldest public park, whose zoo and gardens provided respite for folks of humble status. Gated "townhouse" residences for members of the president's inner circle would replace the verdant park.[101]

After Ben ‘Ali and his entourage took flight in January 2011, throngs of protesters targeted the presidential villas, which were sacked, burned, and photographed with cell phones. But more important, the looted palaces were transformed into political shrines, or pilgrimage sites, where crowds assembled to meditate on and celebrate the fall of the dictator. The revolutionaries also invested many other buildings and spaces with novel symbolic meanings and uses. At the far end of the Avenue Bourguiba in downtown Tunis, the tatty clock tower reconfigured in 1987 to hail Ben ‘Ali's coup was partially dismantled, and it now bears the name of Bou ‘Azizi.[102] Places that had been strictly off limits to pedestrians or shoppers for decades, particularly the sidewalks around the Ministry of the Interior, have been reappropriated for demonstrations, silent vigils, and forums. Sadly, the political murders of two leading members of the Popular Front Coalition called forth yet more commemorative sites. A makeshift shrine in his neighborhood honors the memory of Chokri Belaïd, who was assassinated on February 6, 2013; daily protests were held in front of the Ministry of the Interior to demand justice for his death. On July 25, 2013 (Tunisian Independence Day), Mohamed Brahmi, an opposition member of Parliament, was also gunned down in the streets of the capital. Brahmi's slaying was absurdly incongruous; a leftist, he represented Sidi Bouzid, where it all began. In that town, a furious crowd torched the local headquarters of the ruling Islamist party, Al-Nahda, and the Union Générale Tunisienne du Travail called for a national strike.[103]

The newly energized political role of organized labor in Tunisia explains why a global human rights movement, the World Social Forum (WSF), convened in Tunis in late March 2013 for its first meeting in an Arab country. Some 50,000 visitors from 128 countries gathered for seminars, workshops, concerts, and marches. The WSF—which was originally organized in Porto Alegre, Brazil, in 2001—initially focused world attention on Latin American struggles against authoritarian regimes allied with the International Monetary Fund and other transnational entities. However, a decade later, the Tunisian revolutions resonated with the WSF's expanded global objectives. Climate change had been selected as the WSF's principal theme for 2013, but austerity economics, public and social indebtedness, and human dignity were also on the table. Predictably, women's legal rights proved especially controversial when linked with religion and freedom of expression. Local civil society activists hoped that the WSF would boost the social demand for democracy as the Tunisian secular left wing understands it. Moreover, holding the WSF's meeting in Tunisia drew world attention to the country's part in unleashing not only the "Arab Spring" but also the Occupy Wall Street movements.[104]

The visibility of environmental issues distinguishes current activism in Tunisia from past antiregime mobilization because the degradation of habitats can be publicly debated across the country. The discourse of the environment offers a language for claiming rights in the same way that the lexicon of international human rights had carved out a limited political space for some dissent under Ben °Ali. One alarming consequence of Tunisia's revolutionary years is that industrial pollution has soared. As reported by McNeil and Addala in November 2013, "'In our country, there's no control at all,' says Mohammed, an environmental activist with Kulna Tunis, tossing the empty blue and red shell casings to the ochre sand. 'The el-hbara birds and el-ghzel are being hunted wildly; it is a catastrophe. Companies are taking advantage of Tunisia's weak central authority and deteriorating economy by bringing in hunters to illegally poach gazelles and birds for profit.'"[105] Even worse, as mentioned at the outset, the Gulf of Gabes, a dumping ground for toxic phosphate processing chemicals, has become an ecological disaster zone.

At present, the Tunisian revolutions are complicated by the very mass uprisings that they inspired elsewhere. In Libya the destruction of Muammar Gaddafi's regime and the near collapse of the state have triggered not only refugee flows but also the clandestine circulation of weaponry and fighters across fungible North African borders. Older patterns in the geography of armed resistance have reasserted themselves. The *bled al-siba*, historically situated in the inaccessible terrain of the Chaambi Mountains on the Algerian–Tunisian borderlands, currently shelter Islamist rebels in ways similar to the past.[106]

As unrest on the margins was repressed, an overwhelming majority of assembly members voted for the new Constitution in January 2014. One of the most progressive in the region, the Constitution guarantees equal rights for men and women and state protection for the environment. In the words of the president and head of the National Assembly, Moncef Marzouki, "With the birth of this text, we confirm our victory over dictatorship"; yet he also warned that "much work remains to make the values of our Constitution a part of our culture."[107] The future for the Tunisia of revolution and of "La Tunisie, espace de vacances," still remains uncharted.

Conclusion

Tunisia's characterization as "small, peripheral, and docile" and as "an island of comparative tranquility because it barely casts a shadow beyond its borders" seems not only historically specious but also simply wrongheaded.[108] Scholars of modern Europe now appreciate the historical importance of states other than the usual suspects of territorially massive and/ or imperially mighty nations, such as France, Russia, and Great Britain. In his study of the eighteenth-century Republic of Geneva, Richard Whatmore argues for the centrality of small states' political experimentation; and these same arguments are valid for modern Tunisia.[109] "Small" places thus allow glimpses of imperceptible tectonic shifts transpiring on scales far beyond the "national" level. For the Maghrib, colonialism and nationalism have been cojoined in a tightly choreographed narrative that is both linear and teleological. In consequence, phenomena deemed politically inconvenient, or merely untidy and contingent, were excised or marginalized. As an antidote, this essay proposes an analytical field of vision that captures transnational, weblike forces; transformations; and patterns. It allows historians to factor international congresses, transimperial agrarian development, Mediterranean sports, and global tourism into the story.[110]

It is tempting, and not inaccurate, to seek causation for the revolutions in the moral affronts and social injustices of the late Bourguiba years, and particularly the Ben ⁱAli era. However, this essay's purpose is less to search for immediate triggers and causalities than to propose a conceptual and historical lens that triangulates between spatial displacements, regionalization, and concentrations of power and wealth.[111] Is the notion of coastalization simply another way of talking about state-driven *longue durée* transformations? Or can it move us closer to the fundamental issue—convergence and divergence in multiple, but intersecting, scales?

At one level, the concept beckons historians to define regions, and the assumptions underlying them, using methodologies such as comparative history. I stated above that historical treatments of coastalization in "Greater Tunisia" need to also encompass eastern Algeria and western Libya for certain periods or problems. In addition, changing maritime and sailing conditions tied to systemic climatic variations are relevant. Nautical excavations of sunken vessels lying in the Skerki Banks along the Sicilo-Tunisian Strait, an ancient shipping highway, suggest that sea levels rose during the Little Ice Age. Because they were concealed from view, these dangerous shoals caused more shipwrecks, which reoriented navigation, trade, and passenger traffic. Long-term climatic events, combined with multiple factors, might also have caused the decline of some North African ports to the relative benefit of others.[112] What historians of North Africa need is an archive for studying and assessing cumulative environmental shifts and the human responses to those shifts. For example, state documents, Arabic chronicles, travel narratives, and literary sources can be mined for documentation, albeit fragmentary, for evidence that can be matched with geological, archaeological, and related scientific data.[113]

One argument made here is that historians need to study coastalization and "interiorization" not as discrete phenomena but rather as intersecting vessels, while considering the question of "floating hinterlands" over space and time. In contrast to Algeria, with its relatively compact Berber populations demanding political and cultural autonomy, Tunisia does not have a minority problem, either ethnic (as in Morocco and Algeria) or religious (e.g., the Copts of Egypt). However, I would argue that the Tunisian interior has functioned as an internal or domestic "other," and that the idea of a Mediterranean "personality" can only be instrumentalized by constructing an alternative identity ascribed to the inhabitants of a remote "wilderness," the arid hinterland. (However, the notion of sociocultural estrangement, or even antagonism, between the coasts and interiors has an ancient pedigree dating back to Ibn Khaldun, Rome, and Carthage.)

Lest "the interior" remain in a permanent state of essentialization, it should be noted that its peoples have ceaselessly migrated to coastal cities, and from there often across the sea, to seek work, education, or a political haven, only to return home—or to sink roots elsewhere. Moreover, the interior/coast binary cannot be neatly aligned with the most contentious divide in today's Tunisia—the secular/religious split. And places like Sidi Bouzid can stand in not only for other underprivileged regions in the Middle East and North Africa but also for the semiarid zones that run in a nearly continuous belt across Asia, Africa, and the Americas, and which are currently expanding due to complex human-environmental pressures. Increasingly, if fortune smiles on them, some of the inhabitants of these zones have been fished out of the waters of the Mediterranean, the South China Sea, or the Sea of Cortez, only to be incarcerated in "transition" camps in Melilla, Gibraltar, or southern Arizona.[114] This fact points to future research directions for truly understanding the Arab uprisings or those elsewhere on the planet.

This essay opened with my "sightings" of luxury foreign yachts docked in the marina of Munastir. Among leading French investment groups in Tunisia under Ben ʿAli was the Compagnie Lazard, whose real estate branch is domiciled on the tony Place Vendôme in Paris. Bruno Roger, chairman of Lazard Paris, habitually sailed his yacht to Tunisian ports. In 2006 Imed and Moaz Trabelsi, Ben ʿAli's nephews, reportedly stole the luxury vessel of this well-connected French businessman in a twenty-first-century version of Mediterranean piracy. And this incident, which was widely reported in the French press, sparked an Interpol investigation. The purloined yacht, freshly painted and disguised, was discovered moored in the Sidi Bou Saʿid yacht basin.[115] Explicit connections at all levels of analysis linking transnational corporations and investment (disaster, plunder, or vulture) capitalism with authoritarian political regimes worldwide need to be established. The acclaimed journalist Francis Ghilès, who grew up in Tunisia, noted that in October 2010, the "World Bank gushed with enthusiasm for the country's economic performance."[116]

Much analysis of the current travails of democratization in Tunisia or North Africa still employs a "national" framework that pays insufficient attention to the depth and reach of the global corporate sponsors of dictatorships. It is my hope that original concepts and approaches, such as coastalization, can complicate notions such as globalization, the micro and the macro levels, and regions and regionalization by favoring webs as much as lines.

Notes

1. Habib Bourguiba (1903–2000), independent Tunisia's first president from 1956 until 1987, was a native son of Munastir; for Tunisians, his mausoleum represents a national shrine and pilgrimage site that draws numerous visitors.

2. The United Nations World Tourism Organization projects that by 2020 the number of international tourist arrivals could reach 350 million, with Europe and the Mediterranean as the most popular destinations. See the 2012 UNESCO report that concentrated on Venice, whose experience with mass tourism and rapid climate change holds lessons for the Maghrib; UNESCO, *From Global to Regional: Local Sea Level Rise Scenarios, Focus on the Mediterranean Sea and the Adriatic Sea* (Paris: UNESCO, 2012). There is a substantial literature on mass tourism, pollution, and the Mediterranean; data can be found on the websites of the World Tourism Organization (www2.unwto.org/) and World Wildlife Fund (www.worldwildlife.org), as well as many other sources.

3. In addition, the acute presentist bias in media reporting means that the lion's share of attention now fixates on Islamists and Salafis, which are not unimportant groups, but there are other stories to tell. See Joshua Hammer's excellent analysis of the current state of the Salafi movement: Joshua Hammer, "A New Turn in Tunisia?" *New York Review of Books* 60, no. 12 (July 11, 2013): 13–15.

4. Cyrus Schayegh, "The Many Worlds of 'Abud Yasin; or What Narcotics Trafficking in the Interwar Middle East Can Tell Us about Territorialization," *American Historical Review* 116, no. 2 (April 2011): 273–306.

5. See Diana K. Davis and Edmund Burke III, ed., *Environmental Imaginaries of the Middle East and North Africa* (Athens: Ohio University Press, 2011); and Diana K. Davis, *Resurrecting the Granary of Rome: Environmental History and French Colonial Expansion in North Africa* (Athens: Ohio University Press, 2007). For Cyprus, see Harry Coccossis, "Integrated Coastal Area Management: ICAM Methods and Proposed Strategic Framework," February 2008, www. pap-thecoastcentre.org/pdfs/Web ICAM Report. Needless to say, as is true of any conceptual approach, the notion of coastalization requires interrogation—what are the spatial limits of a human environmental zone deemed "coastal," and how does political ecology determine those limits? And what would taxonomies of "coast" and "coastal" look like, not only for the Mediterranean but also for other world regions?

6. Justin Hyatt, "In Southern Tunisia, Pollution No Longer Swept under the Rug," Inter Press Service News Agency, June 7, 2013, www.ipsnews.net/2013/06/in-southern-Tunisia-pollution-no-longer; Samuel T. McNeil and Radhouane Addala, "Pollution in Gabes, Tunisia's Shore of Death," Al Jazeera, June 14, 2013, www.aljazeera.com/indepth/features/2013/06.

7. *Time* reported the following: "As many as 250 people were missing after a fishing boat overloaded with refugees and migrants from North Africa sank near the Italian island of Lampedusa, located about 70 miles off the Tunisian coast. The island has been overwhelmed by more than 20,000 people fleeing turmoil in Tunisia and Libya"; *Time*, April 18, 2011, 15. See also Elisabetta Povoledo, "Pope Offers Mass on an Island Beacon for Migrants," *New York Times*, July 9, 2013. Human rights organizations claim that at least 1,500 people drowned in the sea in 2011 alone. In 2012 about 500 were reported dead or missing, according to the Office of the UN High Commissioner for Refugees. During the first six months of 2013, an estimated 7,800 migrants and asylum seekers landed on the coast of Italy, often via Lampedusa; most came from Libya

and increasingly Syria, although a good portion were not Libyan nationals but rather expatriate Sub-Saharan African workers.

8. For an interdisciplinary approach to anthropogenic climate change that links the Sahara, Mediterranean, and Atlantic, see Nick Brooks, Isabelle Chiapello, Savino di Lernia, Nick Drake, Michel Legrand, Cyril Moulin, and Joseph Prospero, "The Climate–Environment–Society Nexus in the Sahara from Prehistoric Times to the Present Day," *Journal of North African Studies* 10, no. 3 (2005): 253–92.

9. The notion of a historical tug of war between the *bled al-siba* (zones of tribal or rural resistance) and *makhzen* (areas subordinate to dynastic centers), which shaped the fortunes of the Moroccan state over time, has some applicability to Tunisia in certain periods—particularly when historians reinterpret *siba* and *makhzen* as a continuum, as a complex social field composed of webs of coercion and autonomy, rather than a territorialized binary. One of the first sociological studies in postcolonial Tunisia devoted to the peoples of "the interior" was by Jean Duvignaud, *Chebika: Mutations dans un village du Maghreb* (Paris: Gallimard, 1968).

10. On the problems associated with concepts such as globalization, see the "AHR Conversation: How Size Matters: The Question of Scale in History," *American Historical Review* 118, no. 5 (December 2013): 1431–72.

11. One image of the baguettes as political text from the January 2011 demonstrations is given by Nadia Marzouki, "From People to Citizens in Tunisia," *Middle East Report* 259 (Summer 2011): 16–19. For an analysis of the impact of social media, see Mohamed Kerrou, "New Actors of the Revolution and the Political Transition in Tunisia," in *The Arab Spring: Will It Lead to Democratic Transitions?* ed. Clement Henry and Jang Ji-Hyang (Seoul: Asan Institute for Policy Studies, 2012), 80–99.

12. The most comprehensive analysis of the interconnections between global and local corruption and state repression under the Ben ʿAli regime is given by Béatrice Hibou, *The Force of Obedience: The Political Economy of Repression in Tunisia* (Cambridge: Cambridge University Press, 2011), an expanded and updated version of the French edition, *La force d'obéissance: Economie politique de la repression en Tunisie* (Paris: La Découverte, 2006). See also Camille Le Tallec, "Tunisie: La chasse aux voleurs," *L'Express*, January 13–16, 2012.

13. See, among other works, Alaya Allani, "The Post-Revolution Tunisian Constituent Assembly: Controversy over Powers and Prerogatives," *Journal of North African Studies* 18, no. 1 (2013): 131–40, esp. the chronology, 139–40; and Eric Gobe, ed., *L'Année du Maghreb* (Paris: CNRS Editions, 2011). Gobe's work on the colonial and postcolonial legal profession undertakes such a long-term perspective; see Eric Gobe, "Of Lawyers and *Samsars*: The Legal Services Market and the Authoritarian State in Ben 'Ali's Tunisia (1987–2011)," *Middle East Journal* 67, no. 1 (Winter 2013): 45–63, which is part of his Eric Gobe, "État, avocats, et barreaux en Tunisie de la colonisation à la révolution, 1883–2011," in *Sociohistoire d'une profession politique* (Paris: Karthala-IRMC, 2013).

14. Mehdi Mabrouk, "A Revolution for Dignity and Freedom: Preliminary Observations on the Social and Cultural Background to the Tunisian Revolution," *Journal of North African Studies* 16, no. 4 (2011): 625–35, esp. on the "culture of suicide," 629. See also Amy Aisen Kallander, "Tunisia's Post-Ben 'Ali Challenge: A Primer," *Middle East Report Online*, January 26, 2011, www.merip.org.

15. Thomas P. DeGeorges, "The Social Construction of the Tunisian Revolutionary Martyr in the Media and Popular Perception," *Journal of North African Studies* 18, no. 3 (2013): 482–93.

16. Maamar Sebri offers an invaluable overview of the water regime and associated problems:

Maamar Sebri, "Residential Water Industry in Tunisia: A Descriptive Analysis," *Journal of North African Studies* 18, no. 2 (2013): 305–23, at 305–6. See also Philip McMichael, ed., *Food, Energy, and Environment: Crisis of the Modern World System*, special issue of *The Review* (Fernand Braudel Center) 33, nos. 2–3 (2010): introduction, 95–102. As for tourism to the Mediterranean rim and water consumption, during the summer, when demand skyrockets, the average Spaniard uses an estimated 250 liters per day, while tourists can consume between 440 and 880 liters, the latter amount due to pools and golf courses (these data are from the World Wildlife Fund and World Trade Organization).

17. See the special issue of the *Journal of North African Studies* 19, no. 2 (March 2014), ed. Andrea Khalil, which is entirely devoted to women, gender, and the Arab Spring.

18. John R. McNeill, *Mountains of the Mediterranean: An Environmental History* (Cambridge: Cambridge University Press, 1992); Faruk Tabak, *The Waning of the Mediterranean, 1550–1870: A Geohistorical Approach* (Baltimore: Johns Hopkins University Press, 2008); Edmund Burke III and Kenneth Pomeranz, eds., *The Environment and World History, 1500–2000* (Berkeley: University of California Press, 2009); Julia Clancy-Smith, "Mediterranean Historical Migrations: An Overview," in *Encyclopedia of Global Human Migration*, five volumes, ed. Emmanuel Ness (London: Wiley Blackwell 2013). The most recent work on the social effects unleashed by the onset of the "Little Ice Age" (LIA) is by Geoffrey Parker, *Global Crises: War, Climate, and Catastrophe in the 17th Century* (New Haven, CT: Yale University Press, 2013). There are no studies of this prolonged period of ecological, political, and social crises for North Africa, whose history suffers from a profound indifference to environmental forces, in large measure due to the dearth of or difficulty in finding evidence.

19. Julia Clancy-Smith, *Mediterraneans: North Africa and Europe in an Age of Migration, c. 1800–1900* (Berkeley: University of California Press, 2011).

20. Daniel Panzac, *Barbary Corsairs: The End of a Legend, 1800–1820* (Leiden: Brill, 2005), 139–40.

21. Lucette Valensi, *Fellahs tunisiens: L'économie rurale et la vie des campagnes aux 18e et 19e siècles* (Paris: Mouton, 1977).

22. Kenneth J. Perkins, *Tunisia: Crossroads of the Islamic and European Worlds* (Boulder, CO: Westview Press, 1986), 64–67. Could the (apparently) more frequent harvest failures due to insufficient winter rains during the growing season in the first three decades of the nineteenth century be tied directly or indirectly to the end of the LIA, which had earlier brought wetter summers to the Mediterranean littoral? In the same period the only major river system in Tunisia (and eastern Algeria), the Majarda (Medjerda), underwent a dramatic shift in its course, silting up at least one Mediterranean port, Ghar al-Milh, or Porto Farina, which had played a lead role in the eighteenth-century trans-sea corsair economy. Tabak, in *Waning of the Mediterranean*, had done the most recent research into the effects of the end of the LIA.

23. Mohammed Seghir Ben Youssef gives one of the most detailed portrayals of center–interior relations for the eighteenth century; Mohammed Seghir Ben Youssef, *Mechra El Melki: Chronique Tunisienne du règne des fils d°Ali Turki (1705–1771)*, trans. Mohammed Lasram and Victor Serres, 2nd ed. (Tunis: Editions Bouslma, 1978). Indeed, °Ali Bey (who reigned 1759–82) admitted that the peoples of the interior could retreat to "inaccessible mountains over which I exert little power"; ibid., 442n2. Copies of this unpublished manuscript in various Arabic versions, *Tārīkh al-mashra al-milkī fī salṭanat awlād 'Alī Turkī*, can only be found in the library of the Zaytuna University in Tunis; the author's name would normally be transliterated as Muḥammad al-Ṣaghīr ibn Yūsuf (1691–1771).

Significantly, this chronicle was first translated into French in 1900 and was published by a colonial press in Tunis.

24. On the eighteenth-century marriages concluded with women from the interior and provinces, see Amy Eisen Kallander, *Women, Gender, and the Palace Households in Ottoman Tunisia* (Austin: University of Texas Press, 2013), 45–46.

25. Julia Clancy-Smith, *Rebel and Saint: Muslim Notables, Populist Protest, Colonial Encounters (Algeria and Tunisia, 1830–1904)* (Berkeley: University of California Press, 1994); Mohamed Hedi Cherif, *Pouvoir et société dans la Tunisie de Husayn Bin 'Ali (1705–1740)* (Tunis: Publications de l'Université de Tunis), vol. 2, 181–94.

26. The best study is by Silvia Marsans-Sakly, "The Revolt of 1864 in Tunisia: History, Power, and Memory" (PhD diss., New York University, 2010), which demonstrates the remarkable tenacity and mobilizing power of collective memories and practices of the rebellion among the communities of the "interior," which even today continue to venerate (albeit discreetly) the leader of the revolt.

27. Mohamed 'Ali Habachi, *Les Sahéliens: L'histoire. Documents inédits, archives beylicales et colonials, 1574–1957* (Tunis, 2009), 110–49; Béchir Yazidi, *Le politique coloniale et la domaine de l'état en Tunisie de 1881 jusqu'à la crise des années trente* (Tunis, 2005).

28. See Carmel Sammut, *L'Impérialisme capitaliste français et le nationalisme tunisien* (Paris: Publisud, 1983), 29–39; and Giorgio Riello, *Cotton: The Fabric That Made the Modern World* (Cambridge: Cambridge University Press, 2013). In his analysis of the capitalist and investment potential for agriculture in colonial Tunisia and North Africa, Gaston Deschamps painted a pessimistic picture, mainly due to ecological constraints; Gaston Deschamps, "Vue générale de la Tunisie," in *La France en Tunisie* (Paris: Carré et Naud, 1897), 77–105.

29. Jamil M. Abun-Nasr, *A History of the Maghrib in the Islamic Period* (Cambridge: Cambridge University Press, 1987), 287–97.

30. M. Labidie, "La colonisation française en Tunisie," *La vie technique, industrielle, agricole et coloniale: Numéro spécial, La Tunisie*, May 1923, 9–11. This hesitation to invest was both cause and consequence of the utter incoherence of the early colonial legal systems; see 'Ali Noureddine, *La justice pénale Française sous le protectorat: L'exemple du tribunal de première instance de Sousse (1888–1939)* (Tunis: L'Or du Temps, 2001).

31. In contrast to Algeria, much of the viticulture in Tunisia was carried on either by Italian settlers or by the "White Fathers," a French Catholic missionary order. In a frank scientific (for the period) exploration of Tunisia's rural and agrarian resources and their potential for entrepreneurial development published in 1897, Paul Bourde was ambivalent about future prospects for the capitalization of viticulture; see Paul Bourde, "La culture de la Vigne en Tunisie," in *La France en Tunisie*, ed. Louis Olivier (Paris: Carré et Naud, 1897), 157–60.

32. Habachi, *Sahéliens*; Yazidi, *Politique coloniale*; Julia Clancy-Smith, "A Woman without Her Distaff: Gender, Work, and Handicraft Production in Colonial North Africa," in *A Social History of Women and the Family in the Middle East*, ed. Margaret Meriwether and Judith Tucker (Boulder, CO: Westview Press, 1999), 25–62.

33. This congress, part of the series les Congrès Coloniaux Quinquennaux, was organized by l'Union Coloniale Française. The proceedings were edited by Charles Depincé, *Compte Rendu des Travaux*, 2 vols. (Paris: Siège du Comité d'Organisation du Congrès, 1909). The Torrens Act was defended in vol. 1, 109. However, water and irrigation were clearly matters of concern, indeed alarm, e.g., the discussions in vol. 1, 157–62, of the "great but simple secret of rural prosperity during Antiquity, rural hydraulic installations."

34. For an account of the fervor that the 1913 conference aroused in the eastern Arab world, see Anbara Salam Khalidi, *Memoirs of an Early Arab Feminist: The Life and Activism of Anbara Salam Khalidi*, trans. Tarif Khalidi (London: Pluto Press, 2013), 49–52.

35. See, e.g., the study published during the war years by the noted geographer of North Africa, Augustin Bernard, who observed the apprehensions of French military officialdom regarding recruitment of "colonials" in the army; Augustin Bernard, *L'Effort de l'Afrique du Nord* (Paris: Bloud & Gay, 1916), xvii–10. In contrast to those officials, Bernard lauded the war contributions of North African Muslim soldiers.

36. Mohamed Bash Hamba, "Questions économiques: Prospérité!" in *La Revue du Maghreb* (Genève) 1, no. 6 (October 30, 1916): 181–84; see also Sammut, *Impérialisme*, 356.

37. I detected these transformations from research published by geographers in the period, notably Bernard, *Effort de l'Afrique*; and Augustin Bernard, *L'Afrique du Nord pendant la guerre* (Paris: Presses Universitaires de France, 1926). In the latter work, Bernard signals a profound shift in scientific thinking about the Maghrib's long-term historical and cultural relationship with colonialism—e.g., on p. xiii, he stated that "North Africa is different from the rest of the French Empire because it is attached to Europe and the Mediterranean" by geography and proximity; in a sense, he questioned the Orientalist myth of difference attributed to Islam. In the same period, Jean Grenier, and a group of aspiring writers that included Albert Camus, launched a monthly revue titled *Sud* in Algiers that aspired to debate art and literature with a trans-Mediterranean perspective.

38. Augustin Bernard published a sobering analysis of indigenous rural and demographic conditions; Augustin Bernard, "Le recensement de 1936 dans l'Afrique du Nord," *Annales de Géographie* 46, no. 259 (1937): 84–88. Accounts in radical Algiers newspapers by Camus chronicled the abject misery among the Kabyle peasantry during the postwar period; see Albert Camus, *Algerian Chronicles*, trans. Arthur Goldhammer and intro. Alice Kaplan (Cambridge, MA: Harvard University Press, 2013; orig. pub. 1958). Also, the French anthropologist Germaine Tillion conducted field research in the Aurès and reached similar conclusions; see Julia Clancy-Smith, "La Question de la femme," in *Le siècle de Germaine Tillion*, ed. Todorov Tzvetan (Paris: Editions du Seuil, 2007), 239–50.

39. M. Robinet, "L'École coloniale d'agriculture de Tunis," *La vie technique, industrielle, agricole et coloniale: Numéro special, La Tunisie*, May 1923; Robinet served as the first *directeur de l'école*. See also William Basil Worsfold, *France in Tunis and Algeria: Studies of Colonial Administration* (London: Brentano's, 1930), 108–14. In Paris, a promotional headquarters for the school, the Office du Protectorat Français en Tunisie, was established near the Palais Royal to distribute the official handbook issued by the Direction Générale de l'Agriculture.

40. Worsfold, *France*, 99, 111–13. The School of Colonial Agriculture has not, as far as I know, benefited from scholarly study, due to the tendency of historians of empire in North Africa to neglect the rural or agrarian sectors. It would be significant to know if any Tunisians were enrolled in the school. However, former members of the school, now in France, have formed a society named the Association des Anciens Elèves de l'ECAT.

41. In 1937 Bernard sounded the alarm in "Recensement," 84–87, arguing forcefully that "an augmentation so rapid of the [indigenous] population in a region where cultivable land was restricted" should preoccupy colonial authorities (p. 84); thus a youth "bulge" existed long before the early twentieth-first century. Hafidh Sethom, "La Vie rurale de la Tunisie contemporaine: Etude historique et géographique," *Cahiers de Tunisie* 14 (1966): 203. In strong contrast to the French phobia regarding Italian farmers, the colonial regime preferred Sicilians and other laborers from the Italian Peninsula to work in the phosphate mines in the region of Gafsa. The racial/

ethnic division of labor in the mines created in the 1880s resembled that of petroleum or oil cities in post–World War II Libya—the managerial workers and technicians were all European, while the most dangerous or menial jobs were performed by "natives."

42. In this regard, the post–World War II on-site studies by the French physician and medical geographer Jacques May (aka, Meyer) were ahead of the times; Jacques M. May, *The Ecology of Malnutrition in Northern Africa: Libya, Tunisia, Algeria, Morocco, Spanish Sahara, and Ifni, Mauretania* (New York: Hafner, 1967); for the Maghrib, see 59–63. On p. 59, May noted that in the late 1960s, the Société Franco-Africaine de Marseille still owned 12,000 hectares, including a model modern farming operation with olive groves, wheat fields, and vegetable gardens worth 6 million francs. He also drew attention to the gendered cultural elements creating female and child undernourishment in the interior.

43. Mounira M. Charrad, *States and Women's Rights: The Making of Postcolonial Tunisia, Algeria, and Morocco* (Berkeley: University of California Press, 2001), 214; on the intersections between "land reform" and legal changes to women's status, see 211–15.

44. Sami Bergaoui observes that colonial agriculture drew upon much older more "traditional" forms of labor extraction and land use contracts, "albeit modified and adjusted," which remained in force long after 1956; Sami Bergaoui, "An Aspect of Tunisian Historiography in the Modern and Contemporary Periods: Research in Notarial Archives," in *The Maghrib in Question: Essays in History and Historiography*, ed. Michel Le Gall and Kenneth Perkins (Austin: University of Texas Press, 1997), 212–21. Still useful is the book by Jean Poncet, *La Colonisation de l'agriculture européenne en Tunisie depuis 1881* (Paris: Mouton, 1961). For the Bourguiba era, see Kenneth J. Perkins, *A History of Modern Tunisia* (Cambridge: Cambridge University Press, 2004), 157–76. For the past two decades, see Stephen J. King, *Liberalization against Democracy: The Local Politics of Economic Reform in Tunisia* (Bloomington: Indiana University Press, 2003), where he notes that peasants working small plots had derived some tangible benefits from rural cooperatives. However, "during economic liberalization, agricultural laborers and the small peasantry withdrew from real participation in formal political institutions," retreating into "neo-clientelism" (page 3). See also Stephen J. King, "Economic Reform and Tunisia's Hegemonic Party," in *Beyond Colonialism and Nationalism in the Maghrib: History, Culture, and Politics*, ed. 'Ali 'Abdullatif Ahmida (New York: Palgrave, 2000), 165–93.

45. Maurice Soulié, *La reine scandaleuse: Caroline de Brunswick, reine d'Angleterre (1768–1821)* (Paris: Payot, 1928). Caroline arrived in Tunis with her entourage on April 4, 1816, and spent her days sightseeing until her departure for Athens on April 22. Compare the difficulties and sluggishness of sailing transportation, as detailed by Sir George A. Cockburn, *A Voyage to Cadiz and Gibraltar, Up the Mediterranean to Sicily and Malta, in 1810 & 11, Including a Description of Sicily and the Lipari Islands, and an Excursion in Portugal*, 2 vols. (London: J. Harding, 1815) and by the American consul, John M. Baker, *A View of the Commerce of the Mediterranean: With Reflections Arising from Personal Experience* (Washington, DC: Davis & Force, 1819), with the account of steam travel during the 1860s by James Henry Bennet, *Winter and Spring on the Shores of the Mediterranean: Or, the Riviera, Mentone, Italy, Corsica, Sicily, Algeria, Spain, and Biarritz as Winter Climates* (New York: Appleton, 1870).

46. On tourism to North Africa, see Clancy-Smith, *Mediterraneans*, 147–53. On the Nile Valley, see F. Robert Hunter, "Tourism and Empire: The Thomas Cook & Son Enterprise on the Nile, 1868–1914," *Middle Eastern Studies* 40, no. 5 (2004): 28–54. From 1870 on, Tunisia became the principal site for archaeological work on North Africa in antiquity due to the more or less "scientific methods" (as understood in the period) of the Poinssot family over three

generations as well as the excavations by resident Catholic missionaries. This story is virtually unknown because only very recently, in 2006, were the extensive archival and other documents associated with Franco-Italian archaeology in "Greater Tunisia," or Africa Proconsularis, deposed and catalogued in Paris.

47. Depincé, *Compte Rendu*, vol. 1, 157.

48. Eric T. Jennings, *Curing the Colonizers: Hydrotherapy, Climatology, and French Colonial Spas* (Durham, NC: Duke University Press, 2006).

49. Clancy-Smith, *Mediterraneans*, 153.

50. Thomas Cook, *Tourist Handbook for Switzerland* (London: Thomas Cook & Sons, 1908), 83.

51. Silvia Finzi, ed., *Mestieri e professioni degli Italiani di Tunisia* (Tunis: Éditions Finzi, 2003).

52. E.g., the *Almanach Illustré du 'Petit Parisien'* (Paris, 1930) carried an emblematic piece vaunting the sensual and seductive nature of Algeria that contrasted sharply with the religious tourism organized at the same time in Tunisia. The 1930 Eucharistic Congress has not, to my knowledge, been the subject of an in-depth study. I am currently working on a monograph attempting to disentangle the various strands—in multiple scales and registers—that converged to produce this stupendous imperial miscalculation.

53. 'Ali Mahjoubi, "Le Congrès Eucharistique de Carthage et le mouvement national tunisien," *Les Cahiers de Tunisie: Revue de sciences humaines* 26, nos. 101–2 (1978): 109–32; Kenneth J. Perkins, *A History of Modern Tunisia* (Cambridge: Cambridge University Press, 2004), 89–90.

54. Secrétariat du Congrès, *Livre-guide à l'usage des congressistes* (*Carthage 7–11 mai 1930*) (Tunis: Secrétariat du Congrès, 1930); Mahjoubi, "Congrès."

55. Secrétariat du Congrès, *Carthage 1930: Actes et Documents* (Tunis: Secrétariat du Congrès, 1930), 3–4.

56. Mahjoubi, "Congrès," 111–13; "Catholics at Carthage," *Time*, May 19, 1930, http://content.time.com/time/magazine/article/0,9171,739247,00.html.

57. "Catholics at Carthage."

58. Secrétariat du Congrès, *Carthage 1930*, 37–38, 69–70; Secrétariat du Congrès, *Livre-guide*, 15–22.

59. See Julia Clancy-Smith, "Islam and the French Empire in North Africa," in *Islam and Empire*, ed. David Motadel (Oxford: Oxford University Press, 2014), chap. 4, and James Chappel, "The Catholic Origins of Totalitarianism in Interwar Europe," *Modern Intellectual History* 8, no. 3 (2011): 561–90. Catholic authoritarianism of the 1930s deeply marked politics across Europe in the period and thus trans-Mediterranean connections existed between that authoritarianism and the nature and timing of the Carthage Congress.

60. "Catholics at Carthage."

61. Secrétariat du Congrès, *Carthage 1930*, 192, has a photo of children crusaders. Also see Berque, *North Africa*, 220–21; Charles Diehl, *Les découvertes de l'archéologie française en Algérie et Tunisie* (Paris, 1982); and Mahjoubi, "Congrès," 118.

62. Mahjoubi, "Congrès," 121–32.

63. Pierre-Albin Martel, *Habib Bourguiba: Un homme, un siécle* (Paris, 1999), 23.

64. Omar Carlier made an important point about the critical role played by North African employees of urban tramways in the budding labor movements. Omar Carlier, "Les traminots algériens des années 30: Un groupe social médiateur et novateur," *Le Mouvement Social* 146 (1989): 61–89.

65. Today Tunisia is the world's fifth-largest exporter of phosphoric acid, whose processing has extensively damaged the environment. Nouradin Dougi, *Histoire d'une grande entreprise*

coloniale: La Compagnie des Phosphates et du chemin de fer de Gafsa, 1897–1930 (Tunis: Faculté de la Manouba, 1995). Any full historical discussion of political protest in Tunisia must take into account syndicalism, whose deep roots have made it a force to be reckoned with for nearly a century. However, given space limitations, this essay can only flag trade unionism's tremendous significance—whether in cities, or particularly in the mining regions of the interior—and the early roles played by women in Tunisian syndicalism; e.g., Gladys ᶜAdda (1921–), a labor activist, women's rights activist, and journalist originally from Gabes. Because of its connections to nationalism, a fairly robust scholarly literature exists on the colonial history of syndicalism; to name but a few examples: works by Abdesslem Ben Hamida, including his recent overview "Marginalité et nouvelles solidarités urbaine en Tunisie à l'époque coloniale," *Cahiers de la Méditerranée* 69 (2004): 51–61; and the dissertation by Abdelbaki Hermassi, "Mouvement ouvrier en société coloniale: La Tunise entre les deux guerres" (thèse de doctorat de 3ème cycle, Ecole Pratique des Hautes Etudes, Paris, 1966).

66. Julia Clancy-Smith, "From Household to School Room: Women, Trans-Mediterranean Networks, and Education in North Africa," in *French Mediterraneans: Transnational and Imperial Histories*, ed. Patricia Lorcin and Todd Shepard (Lincoln: University of Nebraska Press, 2014).

67. Taoufik Ayadi, *Mouvement réformiste et mouvements populaires à Tunis: 1906–1912* (Tunis: University of Tunis, 1986).

68. For an important study of the expatriate student Left in France during the postcolonial era, see Daniel A. Gordon, *Immigrants and Intellectuals: May '68 and the Rise of Anti-Racism in France* (Pontypool, Wales: Merlin Press, 2012); and Clement H. Moore and Arlie R. Hochschild, "Student Unions in North African Politics," *Daedalus* 97, no. 1 (Winter 1968): 21–50.

69. In Tunis Père André Demeerseman boldly opposed the Eucharistic Congress in a letter addressed to the archbishop in 1930. Several years later, he stated in writing that "the hour has come for (France) to allow the Tunisian people to take destiny into their own hands," which earned him vicious attacks in the colonial press for being a Tunisian nationalist, which in a sense he was. Born in Belgium, André Demeerseman (1901–1993) began his missionary studies at the White Father novitiate in Maison Carrée in 1922, was sent to Carthage in 1927, and was ordained in 1928; see Francois Dornier, *La vie des catholiques en Tunisie au fil des jours* (Tunis: Finzi 2000), 551.

70. Louis Chauvot, *Le Haut comité méditerranéen et les organismes de politique musulmane* (Paris: Librairie technique et économique, 1937), 29.

71. Ilhem Marzouki, *Le movement des femmes en Tunisie au XXème siècle* (Tunis: Cérès, 1993), 49-52. In May 1931 Habib Bourguiba published a series of articles on famine in *La Voix du Tunisien*, the organ of the nationalist party. He called upon international audiences interested in the "Tunisian problem"—e.g., the International Women's League for Peace and the League of Human Rights—to make connections between human rights and food security; see *Habib Bourguiba: Articles de presse, 1929–1934* (Tunis, 1967), 62–80.

72. See Mark Thomas, *Violence and the Colonial Order: Police, Workers and Protest in the European Colonial Empires* (New York: Cambridge University Press, 2012).

73. Julia Clancy-Smith, "Changing Perspectives on Colonialism and Imperialism: Women, Gender, Empire," in *Historians and Historiography of the Modern Middle East*, ed. Israel Gershoni and Amy Singer (Seattle: University of Washington Press, 2006), 70–100.

74. In contrast, the latest works view women and gender in the colonial situation from a national, imperial, and transnational perspective—e.g., Rebecca Rogers, *A Frenchwoman's Imperial Story: Madame Luce in Nineteenth-Century Algeria* (Stanford, CA: Stanford University Press,

2013); and Sarah Abrevaya Stein, *Saharan Jews and the Fate of French Algeria* (Chicago: University of Chicago Press, 2014).

75. Marie Bugéja, "Ce que fut le Congrès des Femmes Méditerranéennes, Conférence faite à la Société de Géographie, le 7 Juin, 1932," in *Bulletin la Société de Géographie d'Alger et de l'Afrique du Nord* 131 (1932): 544–68. This highly polemic account is the only published narrative of the Congress that I have come across thus far; further research in newspaper collections and colonial as well as feminist historical archives will yield more documentation. See also Julia Clancy-Smith, "L'École Rue du Pacha à Tunis: L'education de la femme arabe et la plus grande France (1900–1914)," *Le Genre de la Nation,* special issue, *Clio: Histoire, Femmes, Société* 12 (December 2000): 33–55.

76. In his massive two-volume work *L'Histoire de l'Algérie Contemporaine,* Charles-Robert Ageron makes no mention of the 1932 Congress, nor do any other general more recent histories of Algeria. Charles-Robert Ageron, *L'Histoire de l'Algérie Contemporaine* (Paris: Presses Universitaires de France, 1979).

77. Huda Sha͑rawi, *Muthakkirat* (Cairo: Dar al-Hilal, 1981); Huda Sha͑rawi, *Harem Years: The Memoirs of an Egyptian Feminist,* trans. and intro. by Margot Badran (New York: Feminist Press, 1986). See also Beth Baron, *The Women's Awakening in Egypt* (New Haven, CT: Yale University Press, 1994); and Marilyn Booth, *May Her Likes Be Multiplied: Biography and Gender Politics in Egypt* (Berkeley: University of California Press, 2001).

78. Once again, to my knowledge, there is no study of this Congress; for an overview of international feminist movements, see Leila J. Rupp, "Transnational Women's Movements," *European History Online,* June 16, 2011, http://ieg-ego.eu/en/threads/transnational-movements-and-organisations/international-social-movements/leila-j-rupp-transnational-womens-movements; and Leila J. Rupp, *Worlds of Women: The Making of an International Women's Movement* (Princeton, NJ: Princeton University Press 1997). Kélani penned a report on the condition of Arab women under the French Mandate, which could not have pleased colonial officialdom: Massara Kélani, "Syria: Extracts from the Report Presented to the Mediterranean Women's Conference in Constantine," *Jus Suffragii* 26, no. 9 (June 1932): 105–6. *Jus Suffragii* was the official monthly journal of the International Alliance, whose members reported worldwide on women's rights, or the lack there of, from as far away as China; the journal regularly reported on Arab women's negative situation under British and French rule in Iraq, Egypt, and Syria.

79. By this period, Bugéja had become a well-known pied-noir writer, polemicist, and advocate for Muslim women's rights in Algeria, for which she lobbied in numerous publications; see Jeanne M. Bowlan, "Civilizing Gender Relations in Algeria: The Paradoxical Case of Marie Bugéja, 1919–1939," in *Domesticating the Empire: Languages of Gender, Race, and Family Life in French and Dutch Colonialism, 1830–1962,* ed. Julia Clancy-Smith and Frances Gouda (Charlottesville: University Press of Virginia, 1998), 175–92.

80. Bugéja, "Ce que fut le Congrès," 546.

81. Ibid., 561.

82. Clancy-Smith, "Islam."

83. On precolonial girls schooling, see Clancy-Smith, *Mediterraneans,* 247–87.

84. al-Haddad, *Imra'tuna fi al-shari͑a.*

85. See Charrad, *States and Women's Rights*; Ilhem Marzouki, *Le Mouvement des femmes en Tunisie au XXè siècle: Féminisme et politique* (Paris: Maisonneuve et Larose, 1993); Nadia Mamelouk, "Anxiety in the Border Zone: Transgressing Boundaries," *Leïla: Revue illustrée de la femme* (Tunis, 1936–40); Nadia Mamelouk, "Leïla: Hebdomadaire Tunisien Indépendant (Tunis, 1940–1941)"

(PhD diss., University of Virginia, 2008); Habib Kazdaghli, ed., *Nisa' wa dhakira / Mémoire de femmes: Tunisiennes dans la vie publique, 1920–1960* (Tunis: Éditions Média Com, 1993); Dalenda Larguèche, ed., *Femmes en villes* (Tunis: Centre de Publications Universitaires, 2006); and numerous other works by Larguèche.

86. Kazdaghli, *Nisa' wa dhakira*.

87. Charrad, *States and Women's Rights*; Marzouki, *Movement*; Kazdaghli, *Nisa' wa dhakira*.

88. Mounira M. Charrad has published the most comprehensive work on the CPS as well as on women in North Africa comparatively and historically. Thus, this section and subsequent sections refer the reader to her magisterial monograph, *States and Women's Rights*, cited above as well as numerous publications, notably Mounira M. Charrad, "Tunisia at the Forefront of the Arab World: Two Waves of Gender Legislation," *Washington and Lee Law Review* 64 (2007): 1513–27; and Mounira M. Charrad and Amina Zarrugh, "The Arab Spring and Women's Rights in Tunisia," e-International Relations, www.e-ir.info/2013/09/04/the-arab-spring-and-womens-rights-in-tunisia/. The quotation is from Charrad and Zarrugh, "Arab Spring," 6.

89. Marzouki, *Movement*.

90. Sophie Bessis, "Le feminisme institutionnel en Tunisie," *Clio: Histoire, femmes et societes* 9 (1999), http://clio.revues.org/286, doi: 10.4000/clio.286.

91. On the CPS, see Charrad, *States and Women's Rights*, 215–32; and Lilia Labidi, "Islamic Law, Feminism, and Family: The Reformulation of *Hudud* in Egypt and Tunisia," in *From Patriarchy to Empowerment: Women's Participation, Movements, and Rights in the Middle East, North Africa, and South Asia*, ed. Valentine M. Moghadam (Syracuse: Syracuse University Press, 2007).

92. Jane Tchaïcha and Khedija Arfaoui, "Tunisian Women in the Twenty-First Century: Past Achievements and Present Uncertainties in the Wake of the Jasmine Revolution," *Journal of North African Studies* 17, no. 2 (March 2012): 215–38; *International Journal of Middle East Studies* 43, no. 3 (August 2011), special section on women and the Arab uprising. See also the important research on women and oral history by Lilia Labidi, *Joudhour al-harakat al-nisa'iyya: Riwayat li-shakhsiyyat tarikhiyya* (Origins of Feminist Movements in Tunisia: Personal History Narratives) (Tunis: Imprimerie Tunis-Carthage, 2009); and Lilia Labidi, *Qamus as-siyar li-l munadhilat at-tunisiyyat, 1881–1956* (Biographical Dictionary of Tunisian Women Militants) (Tunis: Imprimerie Tunis Carthage, 2009).

93. The dean of the Faculty of Letters, Habib Kazdaghli, was only recently acquitted of false accusations of assaulting female students wearing the *niqab* who had forcefully broken into his office, trashing it, in March 2012; see Hammer, "New Turn?" 13.

94. For contrasting uses of Mediterranean universalism across the Strait of Gibraltar, see Eric Calderwood, "The Invention of al-Andalus: Discovering the Past and Creating the Present in Granada's Islamic Tourist Sites," *Journal of North African Studies* 19, no. 1 (2014): 27–55.

95. Omar Carlier, "Medina and Modernity: The Emergence of Muslim Civil Society in Algiers between Two World Wars," in *Walls of Algiers: Narratives of the City through Text and Image*, ed. Zeynep Çelik, Julia Clancy-Smith, and Frances Terpak (Los Angeles and Seattle: Getty Research Institute and University of Washington Press, 2009).

96. Borhane Erraïs, "Archéologie d'un discours politique: Sport et construction nationale, l'exemple Tunisien (1956–1985)" (doctoral état / PhD diss., University of Paris 7 Diderot, 1992). Because of the difficulty in obtaining dissertations from France, I have not yet been able to consult this work.

97. Borhane Erraïs and Marie-Christine Lanfranchi, eds., *Femmes et sport dans les pays*

Méditerranéens, Actes du colloque Euro-Méditerranéen (Antibes: Association femmes, sport, culture, 2001). For references to his numerous publications and a biography of his life, see "Borhane Errais," www.fr.wikipedia.org/wiki/Borhane_Errais.

98. Bill Bramwell, *Coastal Mass Tourism: Diversification and Sustainable Development in Southern Europe* (Clevedon: Channel View Press, 2004). Although sports history is a burgeoning field, there is little scholarship devoted to this important topic. On the Mediterranean Games, see International Committee of Mediterranean Games, www.cijm.org.gr. The games are held every four years, in the year following the Olympic Games; in 2013 Mersin hosted the event.

99. Eric Goldstein, "Before the Arab Spring, the Unseen Thaw," 2011, www.hrw.org/world-report-2012/arab-spring-unseen-thaw.

100. Clancy-Smith, *Mediterraneans*, 288–314. On Bourguiba's despicable behavior toward dynastic and religious elites who posed no threat to his rule or the Republic, see the fascinating account by Francis Ghilès, "North African Diversities: A Tunisian Odyssey," *openDemocracy*, May 22, 2012, www.opendemocracy.net/print/65987.

101. For the US ambassador's lengthy, and quite negative, commentary (from WikiLeaks) on the astonishingly opulent palace in Hammamet occupied by Ben ᶜAli's son-in-law, see Julia Clancy-Smith, "From Sidi Bouzid to Sidi Bou Saᶜid: A Longue Durée Approach to the Tunisian Revolutions, c. 1900–2012," in *The Arab Spring: Change and Resistance in the Middle East,* eds. Mark L. Haas and David W. Lesch, pp. 13–34, Boulder: Westview Press, 2012; and Le Tallec, "Tunisie."

102. Clancy-Smith, "From Sidi Bouzid." The reactions of Ukrainians in February 2014 to the overthrow of Viktor F. Yanukovych were identical. Steven Erlanger reported from Noi Petrivtsi, home to the former president's pleasure palace, that enraged crowds toured the 350-acre estate in the suburbs of the capital city; see Steven Erlanger, "An Abandoned Ukrainian Palace, an Anxious Look toward the Future," *New York Times*, February 28, 2014.

103. Hammer, "New Turn?" 13; Juan Cole, "Tunisia Plunged into Crisis by Second Political Assassinatin," *Informed Comment*, July 27, 2013, www.juancole.com/2013/07/tunisia-political-assassintion.html. See also Carlotta Gall, "Tunisia Says Assassination Had Links to Al Qaeda," *New York Times*, July 27, 2013. It is disquieting that some Tunisians who are invested in, or employed by, the tourist industry have begun now to point an angry finger at "those folks in the interior" for sparking the unrest that has largely ruined the industry.

104. Jon Queally, "As Neoliberal Order Wreaks Havoc, World Social Forum Gathers in Tunisia," March 26, 2013, Common Dreams, http://commondreams.org/headline/2013/03/26-0. See also Medea Benjamin, "A Participant's Account of the World Social Forum in Tunisia," April 3, 2013, http://rabble.ca/news/2013/04/participants-account-world-social-forum-tunisia.

105. Samuel T. McNeil and Radhouane Addala, "Environmental Crimes Run Rampant in Tunisia: Climate Change, Illicit Dumping, and a Two-Year Drought Are Gravely Affecting Tunisia's Landscape," Al Jazeera, November 27, 2013, www.aljazeera.com/indepth/features/2013/11/environmental-crimes-run-rampant-tunisia-201311251180934679.html.

106. The Associated Press in Algiers reported that on March 14, 2014, Algerian security forces apprehended and killed seven militants as they attempted to cross over the border into Tunisia near the city of Tebessa. According to Algeria's Interior Ministry, a large cache of weapons and ammunition was also discovered. See http://lancasteronline.com/news/world/algerian-forces-kill-militants-near-tunisia/article_5b3863e7-f59f-5cc1-b1b2-695ec4000997.html.

107. Al Jazeera and Agencies, "Tunisia Signs New Constitution into Law: Charter May Be One of the Last Steps to Full Democracy after the 2011 Uprising That Sparked the Arab Spring,"

January 27, 2014, http://www.aljazeera.com/news/africa/2014/01/tunisia-assembly-approves-new-constitution-201412622480531861.html.

108. Mustafa Marrouchi, "Willed from the Bottom Up: The Postcolonial Turned Revolutionary," *Journal of North African Studies* 18, no. 3 (2013): 389. Of significance and to contradict what Marrouchi asserts is the fact that Tunisian feminist filmmakers have produced path-breaking documentaries on the revolutions; e.g., see Nadia El Fani, *Neither Allah, Nor Master!* 2011; and Fériel Ben Mahmoud, *Tunisia, Year Zero*, 2011—both at www.IcarusFilms.com.

109. Richard Whatmore, *Against War and Empire: Geneva, Britain, and France in the Eighteenth Century* (New Haven, CT: Yale University Press, 2012).

110. This approach, however, needs to make room for individual life trajectories. For example, the often used monolithic category of "North Africans in France," when teased apart, reveals that students were educational migrants and activists, both male and female, in the Metropole long before empire's demise—but what familial and personal path led them there?

111. The American Historical Association has launched a new series titled Regions and Regionalisms in the Modern World; see Michael Goebel, *Overlapping Geographies of Belonging: Migrations, Regions, and Nation in the Western South Atlantic* (Washington, DC: American Historical Association, 2013).

112. Christian Weitmeyer and Hardi Döhler, "Traces of Roman Offshore Navigation in Skerki Bank (Strait of Sicily)," *International Journal of Nautical Archaeology* 38, no. 2 (2009): 254–80. For the nineteenth century, see Ahmad ibn Abi al-Diyaf, *Ithaf ahl al-zaman bi-akhbar muluk tunis wa 'ahd al-aman*, 6 vols. (Tunis: Al-Dar al-Tunisiya lil-Nashr, 1989), which contains numerous references to unfamiliar climatic patterns; in 1825/1241, the chronicler noted that "a snowfall occurred in the kingdom that was unprecedented (so much so) and the harvest was plentiful . . . and the people (subsequently) referred to this time as the 'year of the snowfall'" (vols. 3–4, 200). The eighteenth-century chronicle by Muḥammad al-Ṣaghīr ibn Yūsuf, *Mechra El Melki*, frequently noted climatic and seasonal events considered out of the norm. E.g., between August 1174 and May 1175 (1761–62), from the fall harvests until spring, "the rain fell without cease, never stopping; the fields were submerged and the grain harvest was lost; few peasants were spared" (p. 445). The chronicle is particularly valuable because the author was *not* from Tunis but rather from Baja, and thus it offers a provincial perspective.

113. On this, see Alan Mikhail, ed., *Water on Sand: Environmental Histories of the Middle East and North Africa* (Oxford: Oxford University Press, 2012).

114. Suzanne Daley, "Africans, Battered and Broke, Surge to Europe's Door," *New York Times*, February 28, 2014. A *New York Times* editorial on Friday, September 19, 2014, page A22, entitled "Murder in the Mediterranean" states that this year has seen a fourfold migratory surge toward Europe's shores compared to 2013.

115. Gregory White, "This Is the Wikileak That Sparked the Tunisian Crisis," January 14, 2011, http://www.businessinsider.com/tunisia-wikileaks-2011-1#ixzz2wXbz1KlD.

116. Ghilès, "North African Diversities."

The Author

Julia Clancy-Smith is professor of history at the University of Arizona; juliac@u.arizona.edu.

Lightning Source UK Ltd.
Milton Keynes UK
UKHW050910020223
416228UK00015BA/174